# Introduction

You have lived multiple lives. At times you have been rich, poor, a servant and a slave. Maybe even a King or a Queen, at the least a member of the minor nobility.

Many famous people in the past have believed in reincarnation, such as Thomas Edison and Sir Arthur Conan Doyle. They both believed in the spirit world and made attempts to communicate with the world beyond.

There is a realm, a universe greater than ours and it is filled with intelligences that we can only wonder at. There are spirits around the earth who are actively helping and guiding us in our planning and during our actual incarnations.

You are interested in this book and in the topic because you know, in your heart, that we are not merely chemical elements that dissolve with death. There must be something more, you know this, because of your own intuition, experiences and beliefs.

There are too many unexplained phenomena for there to be nothing after death. How do some people have past life memories? Why do children remember past lives and then lose the ability after a certain age? How can some people know the future? And more importantly, why do you have premonitions that come true? How could you know what could happen with such certainty?

Reincarnation is a tenet in many religions, such as Hinduism and Buddhism, and is frequently mentioned as parts of varied sects of Christianity and Judaism. It is the concept whereby we have a spirit, in which we retain our central personalities and memories, while in the spirit world, but lose our memories while in a physical form.

This book is here to answer your questions;

1. Why do we reincarnate?

2. How does the process work?

3. How many reincarnations must we have?
4. What memories do we retain from our previous lives?
5. Do we have control over our reincarnations?
6. Why must we suffer?
7. How may I insure my next life is better?
8. How may I progress to being a perfected spirit?

These questions are answered through the Doctrine of Spiritism. In the 1850's, the spirit world determine it was time for the human race to assimilate this knowledge in the hopes it would led us to understand the need to improve our spirituality and to achieve a better balance between our desire for material goods versus our desire to become a more spiritual being.

Explore what is your role and where you are in this journey. Determine your place and your future. Find out the reasons for your current tribulations and how to, not only survive your trials, but prosper through them.

Your journey in different bodies at different times in different circumstances is not without a purpose. You began as a primitive soul and through successive lives, you are being molded into a perfect spirit.

*The Case for Reincarnation – Your path to perfection*

# The Case for Reincarnation

Your Path to Perfection

By

Brian Foster

http://www.nwspiritism.com/

1st Edition

# Table of Contents

# Chapter 1 – Reincarnation – Why is it important?

Why this book? Because now I believe. Others do too. Over twenty percent of Americans believe in reincarnation, including people who are religious and people who aren't.

There is a ground swell of thirst for spiritual awakening throughout the modern world. We have discovered that living in a materialistic culture doesn't satisfy our need to believe and belong to a higher purpose.

The concept of relativism, where there doesn't exist any concept of moral certainty, and unfettered capitalism, where the pursuit of more, at the expense of everything else, as a valued life long process, leave more and more of us cold and unfulfilled. We collectively yearn to be a part of something higher, a cause to make a difference.

Unbeknownst to us, we are part of a plan to make the world better, a plan that started with the formation of the planet. Guided by the spirit world, each one of us is traveling through multiple lives, always with the goal of improving each time. Little steps are accomplished by whole generations, with various calamities in-between, but invariably were marching forward at an imperceptibly slow pace to the objective: a just world.

What that plan is, how reincarnation plays its part and the role that you play is the subject of this book. Yes, you immortal souls, and even though you may not realize it, you are an integral fragment of the whole and without your effort, the plan struggles.

In presenting this plan we must speak of God. Yet the thought of believing in God is anathema to many, because many of us associate that belief with all of the hypocrisy of organized religions, the bigotry  and smugness of those who absolutely *know* we will go to hell unless we believe, pray, dress, act like them. This certainty, this unwavering faith in the unprovable unnerves and repels our rational thinking and thwarts our longing to believe in a supreme power.

We associate a belief in the almighty with simple naiveté; low intelligence that we don't wish to be associated with. The quandary is, if you believe in the spirit world, if you believe in reincarnation, then you return to the question of how can this be? How does this work? Why are we reincarnated?

If speaking of God makes you uncomfortable, then use the label of Divine Force, Supreme Being or Master Intelligence, all words I have read used to denote an organization or an entity setting the dials and pulling the levels which control our destiny. God doesn't mind as long as you have love.

Since we don't wish to have a religious label forced on us, we drift to spiritualism, a vague, amorphous belief that we are able to communicate with spirits. But to what purpose? Why are there spirits wandering around in the first place? This is where Spiritism supplies the how, when, why and where to your questions.

According to Spiritism, there is a plan. Until we delve into the knowledge revealed to us, we shall remain perplexed about the spirit world. We know it's out there; after all there are too many unexplained phenomena for it to be otherwise.

How else do you explain past life memories or the similarities of near death experiences (NDE)? There are simply too many points of unresolved occurrences and testimonials for it to be a simple manifestation of hysteria. We may know a friend or have felt the unexplainable ourselves. Psychologists or other professionals, in dreaming up names like "sleep paralysis" for what happens when we wake with a visitation from a spirit and are unable to move, do little to clarify what actually transpired.

Terms like "sleep paralysis" are conveniences to cover ourselves in jargon. They allow you the distance you need, to not say it must be the workings of another world, a power that is completely unknown to us. And that place must be led by something, where for thousands of years that something has been known as God.

But in your heart you know that it is true that there is a different universe out there, which is, as yet, hidden from our instruments and telescopes. The mind wrestles to reconcile the need for scientific proof versus the inevitability that upon our death, we too shall be one with this alternate state.

It is time to free ourselves of the need to always appear in control and aloof to the mysteries of life beyond death. The stakes are too high to ignore, for there is a world beyond ours, what the Druids called the "Other World". It has been with us before the planet was formed, and we will be part of it after our sun burns out.

The ancients from the priests of Egypt to Greece and Socrates, to the Druids and even the early Christians realized that we travel back and forth from one dimension to the other. They knew it was a requirement for all spirits that in order to grow, to learn, to love, to be fraternal, to participate in a just society, we all have to live many lives to beat out our primitive impulses within us. There are numerous ancient texts and writings hinting at this precept.

Before the advent of Christ, the religious classes of early societies hid their knowledge so they could retain power over the masses, for if people realized the true meaning of the cycle of birth, death, re-birth and on, the ruling hierarchy would quickly see their hold diminish. They could no longer sell their services to promise rewards in heaven, for all would realize that it is a personal process. How we think and act, not an external power anointed only by the priestly nobility, determines our path.

Finally in the 1850's all was exposed. The spirit world, sensing that our culture and technology was ready, disclosed the process of our climb toward perfection. Allan Kardec's codification of "The Spirits Book" was no accident; it was one step in the plan to afford humanity a chance to gain maturity. The revelation was called Spiritism.

## Spiritism

Spiritism burst onto the world scene in the 1850's. Allan Kardec (a penname he was told to use by the spirits), who was not a medium, noticed that when he was present during séances, the mood was serious as opposed to the lighter amusing conversations with more frivolous spirits. Being a methodical person, who wrote text books, taught science classes, and provided free courses to the underprivileged, he arranged a series of questions to be put to the spirit world. Allan Kardec did not just use one medium or one answer. He utilized mediums throughout Europe and didn't include any responses unless he had multiple instances of similar answers from different mediums, all without knowledge of one another.

"The Spirits Book" was the result of his investigation. In it and his four other books is the full context of who we are, why we are here and what our goal in life is.

1. Who we are – We are immortal spirits. How we originated is unknown, even to other spirits, but we know we emerged as primitive intelligence.

2. Why we are here – In our early stages we were placed on primitive worlds to begin to learn the basic lessons of how to survive in a primeval society. We are now on a planet of "atonement", where we reside until we awaken to a higher level of thought. We shed our basic needs for survival and start to grow in our awareness of the needs of others.

3. What our goal is – In our quest to free ourselves of our basic instincts, we are sent to earth to learn the teachings that we require and to learn from our mistakes we made while previously incarnated. The ultimate goal is to reach perfection, but our intermediate goal on earth is to become a well-rounded, loving, and honest person so we may advance to live on a "regenerative" world, where there is social justice and where envy and wars are mostly a thing of the past.

Does Spiritism purport to be a religion? No. According to Wikipedia, "Spiritism is not a religious sect but a philosophy or a way of life by which its followers live. They have no priests or ministers and do not follow any religious rituals in their meetings. They also do not call their places of meetings churches, and instead call them by various names such as center, society or association. Their activities consist mainly of studying the Spiritist doctrine, applying spiritual healing to the sick and organizing charitable missions."[1]

While the study of Spiritism and all of its facets could fill volumes, here we shall concentrate on the full explanation of reincarnation. Without understanding our central role in the entire panoply of the spirit world, the other aspects of Spiritism become mere distant concepts which have no relevance to our daily life.

The big secret is this: we are the entire focus of the spirit world. Our improvements, our successes, our failures, our wars, and so on are the daily concern of the representatives from God, under the leadership of Jesus. Does this focus of attention from powerful beings mean that all of us are valuable? In a way, yes, but in reality they are guiding us with the same concern with which the administrators and teachers of an elementary school love and guide their precious students. Make no mistake; they love us, for all have been in our position before.

## Who Believes

One of the most iconic inventors in American History believed in Spiritism, Thomas Edison. He actively sought ways to communicate with the spirit world. There was an article in the October 1933 edition of Modern Mechanix; "This article purports to have been written about a secret meeting in 1920 in Edison's lab where he tried to communicate with the dead. Complete with illustrations describing how Edison set up a beam projector and photoelectric receiver with delicate instruments that would register anything (including smoke) that would cross the beam's path. This group of scientists sat there for hours and nothing happened."[2]

Thomas Edison worked on various devices to speak to the spirit world until his death in 1931. When he was on his deathbed, the following was purported to have occurred; "Before dying,

Edison briefly came out of his coma and said to his wife, Mina, who was keeping vigil at his bedside, and his doctor that "It is very beautiful over there!"[3]

Sir Arthur Conan Doyle, the author of the Sherlock Holmes series of stories, was a believer in Spiritism. He wrote a novella, *The Land of the Mist*, that revolved around spiritualism and he wrote a book, *The History of Spiritualism*, in 1926. In it, he devoted a chapter to Allen Kardec's Spiritist Doctrine.[4]

He attended séances to further his communication with the spirit world; however certain mediums took advantage of him and used tricks to fake conversations with the dead. He attended at least one séance with the wife of Dr. Carl Wickland, the chief psychiatrist at the State Psychopathic Institute of Chicago[5], who was a believer in the spirit world even though he did not believe in reincarnation.

Another major 20th century figure who believed in spiritualism, not particularly in Spiritism, was Carl Jung. He recognized the need to identify one's life as part of God's plan. He would recommend that some patients pursue spiritualism to assist their journey for a cure. In fact, "Jung recommended spirituality as a cure for alcoholism and he is considered to have had an indirect role in establishing Alcoholics Anonymous. Jung once treated an American patient (Rowland Hazard III) suffering from chronic alcoholism. After working with the patient for some time and achieving no significant progress, Jung told the man that his alcoholic condition was near to hopeless, save only the possibility of a spiritual experience. Jung noted that occasionally such experiences had been known to reform alcoholics where all else had failed."[6]

There are many instances of well-known rational and highly intelligent people who believe in an unseen world that lies amongst us, a world that Francisco C. Xavier, also known as Chico, who was recognized as Brazil's greatest medium, said begins at the tip of our nose.

## Why I believe

At the beginning of the book, I said I wrote this book because now I believe it. I want to focus on the workings of reincarnation and not on myself in this book. Suffice it to say, I am not one who had a near death experience or even a personal spiritual encounter. Nor was I even of a religious inclination to begin with. I grew up going to the Episcopal Church, although my parents stopped going early on and of course I did too. Needless to say, I much preferred my Sundays to myself, playing with my friends.

My parents were friends with the Reverend of our Church and we used to be together at a beach house for a week or so at a time. I do remember him as the nicest man and I have never met a kinder, gentler person in my life since. Plus, and this is a test for many, all of his children were wonderful people.

I came to Spiritism because of a journey of discovery. I was driven to ascertain how the future could be foretold. If the future is known, then we don't live in a non-deterministic universe, but one where the term fate has meaning. Our random collection of life experiences are not really random, but must have been planned or even possibly guided.

My wife was told of certain events to happen in the future, more than fifteen years before we would meet. Extremely specific events did occur, which could, in the scheme of things be mathematically possible but certainly not probable. One instance foretold the consequences of the Great Recession of 2007-2008. Very personal events unfolded that I did not believe at the time, even though my wife told me, in advance, the exact sequence which would occur.

Unfortunately, I wasn't smart enough to write down the prophecies and put them in escrow for proof. I have no physical evidence whatsoever, only my desire to understand how someone could, with no knowledge of the American banking system, be so accurate.

Once the covers are partially pulled back to reveal a mystery, all other preconceptions must be re-analyzed. This is where I stood, profoundly affected; my haughtiness of thinking that I was the master of my own destiny was shattered. Something out there had power over me; over me! Not an impersonal God, who I once thought may be some remote divinity that had most probably had forgotten about us here on earth. After all, weren't we created from random flotsam and jetsam that combined into amino acids, then proteins and took off from there?

To be clear, the Spiritist Doctrine does say we are the product of evolution from primordial elements. However it clarifies that the earth was guided in its evolutionary path. Humans were always in the plan.

The search for how I could have been manipulated (or so I thought) into taking the steps to lead me where events foretold came true brought me, finally, to Spiritism. After researching countless other ideas, such as the theory that the universe is a hologram and we are actually like a DVD where you can fast forward and reverse but the actors can only play the part that was selected, all left me cold. Only when I first started reading *The Spirits Book*, in pdf format on the web, did I then have my moment of clarity, for not only is the question of pre-determination answered, but the entire reason for the world being as it is, is explored and explained.

In the Doctrine of Spiritism, one of the central tenets is reincarnation. The presence of reincarnation explains why we are reborn and for what purpose. By fully realizing that purpose, you will comprehend why your life has played out in the fashion that it has. You shall understand the bad times were necessary. You will perceive that whatever situation you find yourself in, there is always a solution, because no trial is created without the possibility of victory. Old age won't mean that our wishes and ambitions must be buried as unattainable. Lastly, the looming specter of death won't be seen as a tragedy, but as a new beginning and one more step toward perfection.

# Chapter 2 - Why Believe in Reincarnation

Many religions teach their adherents about the existence of reincarnation, but why does Spiritism, in particular believe in it? Spiritism considers that the early Christians also professed knowledge about our souls reincarnating, but this belief dissipated over the centuries after Christ. Spiritism renews the teachings of Christ and supplements them with the revelations promised to us, revelations that first appear in the New Testament.

> "If you love me, keep my commands. And I will ask the Father, and he will give you another Consoler to help you and be with you forever...the Spirit of truth. The world cannot accept him, because it neither sees him nor knows him. But you know him, for he lives with you and will be in you." New Testament John 14: 15-17

> "But the Consoler, the Holy Spirit, whom the Father will send in my name, will teach you all things and will remind you of everything I have said to you." New Testament John 14: 26

What did the Consoler actually do? What did the Spirit of Truth contribute? Spiritism states that Allan Kardec was the Codifier, who presented, via mediums throughout Europe, the Spirit of Truth (Consoler) and that in the five books that Allan Kardec assembled, he revealed the extent of the Spirit world, whats God is, who Jesus is, why we are here on earth, how we should live and the doctrine to follow. That is all. Within those books are the reasons why we reincarnate.

If one looks at the vast literature written about reincarnation, covering our past lives, childhood memories of past lives, as well as hypnotically obtained revelations that some people lived on other planets, there seems to be many disjointed facets. In truth, however the general principles correspond with the Spiritist teachings. To understand the sweeping field of literature out in the world today, one should review the concept of reincarnation presented by Spiritism, and then all becomes clear. Spiritism provides the context, the rules, the process and the endgame for our multiple lives.

## Reincarnation According to Spiritism

The Doctrine of Spiritism maintains that the goal of God and Jesus is for all us, as children of God, to become pure spirits. Each of us, through our own efforts, slowly advances toward the perfection of God. We will never reach the goal of absolute perfection, but we should come as close to pure love and harmony within the universe as possible. We are all immortal spirits; therefore we have until the end of time for our journey.

An example of a pure spirit is Jesus. He is one who truly loves us with all of his fiber, who understands the trials we must endure, our failings, our weaknesses, our petty jealousies, yet even still radiantly smiles down upon us, knowing that someday we shall become wholly integrated within the loving universe and take our places as a force for good.

The central question is: how do we become pure? The answer lies within *The Spirits Book*;

> *166. How can the soul that has not attained perfection during the corporeal life complete the work of purification?*
>
> "By undergoing the trial of a new existence"
>
> *How does the soul accomplish this new existence? Is it through it transformation as a spirit?*
>
> "The soul, in purifying itself, undoubtedly undergoes a transformation; but, in order to effect this transformation, it needs the trial of corporeal life"
>
> *The soul has then, many corporeal existences?*
>
> "Yes; we all have many such existences. Those who maintain the contrary wish to keep you in the same ignorance in which they are themselves."

*It would seem to results from this statement that the soul, after having quitted one body, takes another one; in other words, that it reincarnates itself in a new body. Is it thus that this statement is to be understood?*

"Evidently so."[7]

Therefore, to ascend we must accept the task of being reborn in a physical body. There are lessons that only can be learned through a bodily existence. But why do we need to reincarnate multiple times?

## The Need for Multiple Lives

Multiple lives are required, because one life alone doesn't supply all the lessons needed for us to ascend. The spirit Andre Luiz, wrote many books, psychographed by Francisco C. Xavier, in which he goes into great depth about various aspects of the spirit realm. In one book, he explores the need for us to be reborn over and over again. Andre Luiz was assigned to a group of spirits who assisted people leaving their earthly life in the book, *Workers of the Life Eternal*, where he underwent numerous experiences at people's bedsides and witnessed the dramas that swirled around them. He weighs the frequent scenes and stories of people struggling to depart and comes to the conclusion;

> "Studying cases of death had enriched my knowledge in the field of mental science. The spirit, (eternal in essence) makes use of matter (transitory in its associations) as didactic material that evolves more and more in the spirit's never ending course of experience toward integration within the Supreme Divinity."[8]

What does Andre mean by didactic material in this instance? One of the definitions of didactic is "Teaching or intended to teach a moral lesson."[9] Therefore as we continue learning in the Spirit world and travel through various physical trials on earth we accumulate moral lessons that in turn influence our physical bodies and the structure of our brain, as we are reborn. Not only is our intellectual being as spirits important, but the physical makeup of our human form is vital for our involvement on our planet and for our eventual elevation as spirits.

Given all that he had seen, Andre fully realizes the need for our multiple attempts at learning in our corporeal bodies, "Hence the reasons for the complex activities of the evolutionary road, the countless diversities, the multiplicity of social positions, the degrees of abilities and the levels of intelligence on the various planes of life."[10] What a wonderful revelation! We all go through periods of high social positions, living life with riches, and being the smartest person in the room. Although, we also live in the opposite positions. Truly, this knowledge must cause us all to be humble.

Being trapped in a material body affords us the opportunity to learn what is not possible to apprehend in the spirit world. While certainly, one can gather intellectual knowledge, the building of our emotions, of faith, charity, honor and love are rooted in the pain and suffering we are exposed to in the physical world. *The Spirits Book* backs up this thesis, in the secondary question to question 175;

> *Would it not be happier to remain as a spirit?*
>
> "No, no! For we should remain stationary; and we want to advance towards God."[11]

For those who believe we only need one physical life to be pure, it is as if we wanted to be the President of a large company without ever working any other job. Of course we must start in the mail room and work our way up in various positions to fully comprehend how things get done and how to survive within the culture of the organization. No matter how pious we could have started out as a new spirit, we would still need the required know-how to gain our elevation. Only through rigorous trials do we have the right mixture of beliefs and knowledge to reincarnate with good prospects of success and to be a valued worker in the Spirit realm.

## Multiple Lives – Where?

Hence, we do need to accumulate a mountain of instances and encounters from all social, cultural, and physical environments. We are on task to build a strong foundation, upon which we can amass ever more knowledge and possess the wisdom to utilize it appropriately. So where do we begin to lay the base for our future? The answer, once again, lies in *The Spirits Book*;

> *172. Do we accomplish all our different corporeal existences upon this earth?*
>
> "Not all of them, for those existences take place in many different worlds. The world in which you now are is neither the first nor the last of these, but is one of those that are the most material, and the furthest removed from perfection."
>
> *173. Does the soul, at each new corporeal existence pass from one world to another or can it accomplish several existences on the same globe?*
>
> "It may live many times on the same globe, if it be not sufficiently advanced to pass into a higher one."
>
> *We may, then, re-appear several times upon the earth?*
>
> "Certainly."
>
> *Can we come back to it after having lived in other worlds?"*
>
> "Assuredly you can; you may already have lived elsewhere as upon the earth."[12]

The answers imply that we live on whatever worlds may be necessary, in order to gather the required curriculum. We are all interstellar travelers, but alas, our memories of our journeys are hidden from most of us. We regain those thoughts and remembrances when we return to the spirit world.

## Where are we heading?

Where does all of this lead to? Are we locked into paying for our wrongs and learning lessons the hard way forever? No. At some time in our future existence, when we have built a foundation of experiences that enable us to gather more knowledge and retain our humbleness and capacity to love, without any urge to act superior, our next step is to be promoted to a world of regeneration.

The worlds of regeneration are described in Allan Kardec's *The Gospel According to Spiritism*;

> "Regenerative worlds serve as a transition between worlds of expiation and worlds of bliss. The repentant soul finds peace and repose on them and ends up purifying itself. Of course, on such worlds humans are still subject to the laws that govern matter; their humanity still experiences your sensations and desires but is free of the muddled passions that enslave you; on regenerative worlds there is no longer the pride that renders your heart silent, the envy that tortures it and the hatred that suffocates it. The word love is written on every brow, a perfect equity governs social relationships, and all acknowledge God, endeavoring to evolve toward him by following his laws."[13]

Regenerative worlds are but one stop. There are more advance worlds that await us as we climb up the ladder to perfection. Most certainly, the description of a regenerative world is one of an earthly paradise to us. Though we must reincarnate, our lives in such a world will not be as brutish and full of drama that tears away at our quest to be calm. This is a world where one can be happy and free to focus on the education that we agreed to before being reborn.

As one can see, there is no shortcut. No payment can be made to the right person to skip our trials. After all, a child can't become an adult in an instant. Even though that child may be an extraordinary genius, the child must still grow emotionally so that he or she can focus his or her intellectual energies at the right target. To all of us here, reading, at this very moment, we are all the same. The variations that we perceive to be so great are but minuscule to an observer from the spirit world. We are but a mass of unruly students, learning how to behave in an adult's world.

Now that we know why we are subject to the reincarnation process, it is time to explore how it works.

# Chapter 3 - How Do We Tie Our Spirit to Our Body?

You may ask, how does reincarnation really work? How can we know who we are in successive lives and in the spirit world? The answer is the perispirit. The perispirit is the part of us that combines with our purely physical body at birth and detaches from the latter upon death. We retain our perispirit, until we reach the level of a pure spirit, which at such time, we become pure energy. There are more detailed explanations in other Spiritist books, but for a quick and relatively comprehensive summary, this chapter is a good beginning.

In the book *Between Heaven and Earth*, by the spirit author Andre Luiz, there is a quick summary of how the perispirit controls our physical body. The corresponding passage below describes team of spirits examining a male spirit named Julio, who had poisoned himself while incarnated on earth. Now, even as a spirit, his throat is an area of pain. The team leader Clarencio, explains the now discarnated spirit's problems. In order for them to understand Julius' case, however, he first begins with this explanation about the impact of thought on the physical body, by way of the perispirit's force centers:

> "Whatever the corruption of the thought is, such will be the disharmony in the particular force center that reacts in our body to this or that class of mental inflow. Let's apply earthly terminology to our short lesson as much as possible so that you can better grasp what we are saying. As we analyze the physiology of the perispirit, we may classify its force centers by remembering the most important areas of the physical body. Thus, using the best expression for the vehicle that serves us presently, there is the 'crown center', which, on earth, is considered by Hindu philosophy as being the thousand-petal lotus and the most important center of all due to its high radiation potential and its connection with the mind, the shining seat of the consciousness. The crown center receives, first of all, the stimuli of the spirit, commanding other centers,

yet vibrating with them in a perfect system of interdependence. Considering in our exposition the phenomena of the physical body, and satisfying the imperatives of simplicity in our definitions, we can say that the energies of nourishment for the nervous system and it subdivisions emanate from this center, providing all the electromagnetic resources that are indispensable for organic stability. Therefore, it is the great assimilator of the solar energies and rays from the Higher Realms that can favor the sublimation of the soul. Next, there is the 'cerebral center', contiguous to the 'crown center', and which orders the various types of perception, which in the physical body, comprise sight, hearing, touch and the vast network of the processes of the mind that have to do with Speech, Learning, Art and Knowledge. It is in the 'cerebral center' that we possess the command of the endocrine center, which has to do with the psychic powers. Next, there is the 'throat center', which presides over the vocal phenomena, including the activities of the thymus, the thyroid and the parathyroid. Then, there is the 'heart center', which sustains the services of the emotions and overall equilibrium. Proceeding on down, there is the 'splenic center', which, in the dense body, is seated in the spleen and regulates the distribution and circulation adequate for the vital resources in every corner of the body. Then, comes the 'gastric center', which controls the entrance of nourishment and fluids into the body, and lastly is the 'genesic center', housing the sanctuary of sex as a molding temple of forms and stimuli."

"But we mustn't forget that our subtle vehicle, like the physical one, is a mental creation on the evolutionary pathway, woven out of resources taken temporarily by us from the storehouse of the universe. It is a vessel that we utilize to house the divine light of sublimation in our eternal spirit. Everything is the work of the mind in time and space, making use of thousands of forms in order to become purified and sanctified for the Divine Glory."[14]

## Force Centers

This was a lot to review; here is a table with the listed centers;

1. Crown Center – Command all other centers. The stimuli of the spirit. Assimilates and distributes solar energies and electromagnetic resources.

2. Cerebral Center – Controls senses, sight, hearing, touch, psychic abilities.

3. Throat Center – Controls speech.

4. Heart Center – Controls emotions.

5. Splenic Center – Controls the distribution of nourishment for your body.

6. Gastric Center – The entry point of food and fluids.

7. Genesic Center – Controls sex and allows stimulus to your body.

Therefore, the perispirit is composed of seven major centers, all working in concert to regulate our spiritual and physical bodies. One could imagine the perispirit lying as a transparent layer inside our bodies, connected to our material organs to guide, heal and regulate our physical life. The connection is a two way street, as we live and learn in our bodies, the perispirit absorbs feedback, allowing it to transfer the knowledge gained in our present life to be used in the spirit world and our subsequent lives.

## Chakras

The seven force centers correspond to the seven major Chakras in the Hindu and Buddhist tradition. Chakras are energy points in the "subtle body". The "subtle body" is not part of the physical body but is part of a different plane of existence.[15] Therefore, the "Subtle body" corresponds to the perispirit.

Hence the eastern religions knew of the vehicle that contains our spirit while we are here in the physical world. They understood that we are but travelers here on earth, taking our turn living as dense matter, so we may partake of physical life what has been assigned to us.

## What Happens in the Next Life, When One Center is Affected?

Let us return to Julio, the one who poisoned himself, his throat is an object of pain for him even in the Spirit world. How will he repair his pain and his sin of suicide? Again the learned Clarencio explains;

> "When by acts contrary to the Divine Law, our mind harms the harmony of any one of our soul's force centers, it is naturally enslaved to the effects of the unbalancing action, thus making the toil of readjustment necessary. In Julio's case, he is the author of disturbance in the 'throat center', an alteration expressed by an infirmity or imbalance that will by necessity go with him into reincarnation."
>
> "How will he cleanse the deficiency?" I asked (Andre Luiz, author of Between Heaven and Earth), edified by the explanation I had just heard.
>
> "Julio will have to live with pain in his throat, thus healing himself by correcting the vibratory tonus of the 'throat center' and reestablishing it to normality."
>
> "Julio will be reborn in a physiologically defective body, which will somehow portray the injured area, his throat. He will suffer intensely from the vocal organ, which will undoubtedly be characterized by weak resistance to microbial attacks. In virtue of our friend having scorned the blessing of a physical body, he will be faced with dreadful struggles in order to learn how to appreciate it instead."[16]

All deficiencies are carried over with us, from one life to the next. Whichever part of the body we abuse in one life will be affected in the next. Socrates, the ancient Greek philosopher, knew what he was talking about when he said, “Everything in moderation, nothing in excess”, over 2500 years ago. Keep in mind the seven centers, and check your excesses. If you are having problems in one or more areas, then you should know exactly what to work on in your present life. This is reinforced by one of the team members commenting to Clarencio, “So, we must attribute an important role to infirmities in the human realm because most of them play an important role in the regeneration of souls.”[17]

The statement above contradicts all that we modern humans have learned. We are told sickness is caused by viruses, bacteria, and other environmental factors alone, having nothing to do with own behavior. To believe so puts us back in the eras of superstition. Back then, when an ailment occurred, the first thing a person would ask is, “Why is God punishing me?” or “What did I do wrong to deserve this?” Could there be, perhaps, truth in the real cause of our troubles? Are we then supposed to ask, when a bad illness strikes us, “What should I improve in my life to not have this occur again?” The answer is a qualified “Yes”.

Although, as taught by Spiritism, viral and bacterial infections can still occur naturally and thus we are encouraged to use the services of medical professionals when we have any problems. The vital point is that the spirit world knows all, even each effect of our scientific advances, including what can be cured and what can’t be cured. We are programmed in our new life to experience trials; each trial is arranged with whatever assistance we may have from medicine taken into account.

## All Must be Brought into Harmony

Because of the imbalances that develop, each center must be calibrated and re-measured periodically. As Andre Luiz says, “Each ‘force center’, must be brought into complete harmony with the Divine Laws that govern us so that we can ascend toward Perfect Equilibrium.”[18]

What are the main causes of our diseases? Clarencio supplies the answer: “Pride, vanity, tyranny, selfishness, laziness and cruelty are vices of the mind that generate disturbances and diseases in its instrument of expression."[19] Unfortunately, even if we have conquered all in our present life, we may have been destined to have a trial of illness for a wrong doing in a past life. Therefore, as we suffer through bad periods, the best strategy is to always seek medical help, maintain a good attitude, refrain from blaming other people, and meditate on how to improve ourselves.

When, during our life here on earth, we persist in the errors of selfishness and other wrongs, the affect carries on in our perispirit. Whatever we did incorrectly will harm one or more of our force centers, causing a breakdown in the harmony of our perispirit. Clarencio details the effects and the remedy:

> "Infirmity, as disharmony of the spirit continues on in the perispirit. Known diseases, in addition to others that have escaped human diagnosis, will persist for a long, long time in the tormented spheres of the soul, leading us to readjustment. Pain is the great, blessed remedy. It reeducates our mental activity, restructuring the pieces of our instrumentation and polishing the animic centers that our mind uses to develop itself on its journey toward the life eternal. Aside from the power of God, pain is the only force capable of altering the course of our thoughts, compelling us to make indispensable changes with a view to the Divine Plan for us, the execution of which we cannot avoid without grave harm to ourselves."[20]

The remedy is pain. When we are in error, we endure discomfort. As we train our children, with a gentle spank, when they do something that could be life threatening, the small amount of pain is meant for them to focus on the undesirability of performing that action again. Well, the same goes us. When we are in pain, think of what we could have done to deserve the punishment, then think of how to train ourselves to not perform that action anymore in this or the next lifetime.

The conduit of experiences flowing from one's life on earth to the spirit realm to the next life on earth is the perispirit. In *The Gospel According to Spiritism*, we are told, "God has given us for our advancement precisely what is necessary and what will be enough for us: the voice of conscience and our instinctive tendencies, taking from us what could harm us."[21] Therefore the perispirit guides us in our conscience and instincts when we are here on earth and absorbs new lessons to carry us through the next life, honing our instincts to know what is the right thing to do and what circumstances to avoid. The voice of our conscience becomes stronger and more accurate as we acquire new proficiencies. The perispirit is the vehicle in which we must ride in our eternal quest to become an elevated spirit.

Now that we have learned that the perispirit is what we are contained in when we reincarnate, the next question is how the perispirit associates itself with a new born child.

# Chapter 4 - Preparation for Birth

What happens at the moment of conception, or later while the fetus grows in the womb? Depending on the past life and the importance of the mission the amount of assistance given by the Spirit world differs. The process is described in the book *Between Heaven and Earth*, dictated by Andre Luiz to Francisco C. Xavier.

## Entering the Womb

How does the perispirit enter the mother's womb? In the book *Between Heaven and Earth*, there is a scene where there is a plan for a child to be born to a couple. The mother-to-be (Zulmira) is brought into the spirit world, during her sleep, to meet her child. She demonstrates great love for her child and is excited to have a baby boy. During the next night a group of spirits is outside the bedroom of Zulmira and her husband, waiting for them to finish their act of conception. When the couple have fallen asleep, the spirits enter the room. They assist Zulmira out of her body to receive the child. The action of Zulmira embracing and placing her son into her womb is described;

> "From then on, Zulmira seemed fully concentrated on the boy, who entwined himself with her like a mollusk accommodating itself to its shell."
>
> "Held on the maternal lap, he seemed to immerse himself into it."[22]

Andre Luiz, the spirit author of the book who was a member of the group helping the joining of the mother and the son, analyzes the process;

> "On other occasions, I had witnessed the preparatory steps of reincarnation, which required the active concourse of technicians specializing in the process, along with benefactors from the higher life; but this time, the phenomenon was very simple. As it juxtaposed itself on the delicate tissues of the mother's perispirit, the boy's own subtle body gradually shrank

before our eyes."[23]

## Exceptional Births

Andre Luiz is curious. Why didn't he see the larger number of technicians at Julio's (the baby boy) conception as he did at others? His team leader explains;

> "Julio's reincarnation won't require any special attention from our sphere. It is an experimental descent into the arena of dense matter and is of interest only to himself and his family members. However, if his life were meant to influence society as a whole, and if he were the holder of indisputable merit with responsibilities toward others, the matter would be quite different. Forces of a higher order would be fatalistically mobilized to interfere with his chromosomes to ensure that the embryo would be suitable for its mission."[24]

The extent of guidance of the Spirit Realm into the affairs of our earthly existence is remarkable. The process of a normal reincarnation, where a spirit is re-entering the world to learn and to atone for past sins, is a thing of beauty. The act of having the mother meet her child beforehand, to ensure the love and devotion required to raise a new life into this world is a wonderful gift given to us by God. But, the revelation that for special lives, those spirits that are marked by the spirit realm to contribute to humanity, are carefully engineered. From their inception, each detail of their DNA is guided to produce a child of inborn talent. A miracle which answers many questions when we see children of exceptional merit.

Andre Luiz and his fellow teammate (Hilario) probes deeper into the process of interference with an embryo;

> "What if the reincarnating spirit were a man of broad intellectual powers?" asked Hilario.
>
> "We would have to pay special attention to the brain structure so that he would be ensured of having an instrument capable of enabling him to fulfill his duties involving the materialization

> of thought", replied Clarencio (the team leader)
>
> "What if he were to be a doctor? A great surgeon, for example?" I asked in turn.
>
> "He would receive special assistance in the development of his nervous system to ensure that he had complete control over his emotions."[25]

We are being told of the active manipulation of countless births throughout our history to direct our species to the ultimate goal of assisting human society to achieve the next step of evolving into a better world. How like children we are! Being gently directed into paths for our own good, all the while clueless and absorbed into our selfish existence.

## Starting Over Again

After such a revelation, Clarencio describes the vast majority of reincarnations;

> "However, embryonic principles function automatically in thousands of rebirths every day. The law of cause and effect does its work without any need for management on our part. In reincarnation, all that is needed is the parents' magnetism, combined with the strong desire of the one who is returning to the arena of physical forms. When we return to the physical body, we are invariably animated by a firm purpose ... whether it be the desire to relieve the pain that torments us, the longing for spiritual victories that facilitate our entry to the Higher Life, the vow to recapitulate unfulfilled responsibilities, or the ideal to accomplish great endeavors of love amongst those with whom we have an affinity. Generally speaking, most souls that reincarnate satisfy the restless desire to start out again. Those who haven't taken seriously enough the endeavor that life has entrusted to them quickly yield to the imperative to repeat the experience, and their reentry into the physical struggle appears as a redemptive blessing. Millions of destinies are restructured like that, like a huge forest being replanted. A seed grows, simulated by the magnetism of the soil; a corporeal existence

germinates anew, stimulated by the magnetism of the flesh."[26]

Such are the laws of nature of which we here on earth have no insight. We explore the known material world for rules and express them as mathematical laws, but as yet we little understand the law of cause and effect and how we are buffeted by its winds every day, every minute of our lives. From our time as spirits to our multiple incarnations we are pushed onto a path of redemption and the miracle of birth facilitates our journey.

# Chapter 5 - Childhood

Now that we know how the perispirit is placed in the fetus, we need to explore how childhood evolves.  Do we remember who we were, what we did? Why must we endure childhood? How do we keep our individuality through the first stage of our life? The process is fully explained by Spiritism.

Additionally, Spiritism answers questions such as: if God is all powerful, why must we be infants and children first? If we truly need to come to earth to learn from our past mistakes, wouldn't it be easier to come as an adult and start the process? To start, let's examine what Jesus taught us:

> At the time Jesus said, "I praise you, Father, Lord of heaven and earth, because you have hidden these things from the wise and learned, and revealed them to little children. Yes, Father, for this was your good pleasure." (Matthew, chapter 11:25)

As with many passages in the Bible, this could be interpreted in different ways. According to the doctrine of Spiritism, the most likely answer is that little children represent our humble aspect. As children we looked up to our parents, gladly taking in what they offered us, without question and with the trust of innocence. This is different from the stage of being a teenager, questioning everything and secretly (or not so secretly, depending on their mood) thinking that we know best and everyone else is irretrievably stupid. Hence, we should accept the Word of God as children accept the word of their parents. We should have faith that this love will see us through and that we shall become wiser with age, while the foundation of our moral code is strong, stable, and everlasting.

What was hidden from the wise and learned? First, the attitude of humility, the recognition that we have little knowledge, that we always have more to learn. Next, the fact the Universe does not rotate around us, but that we must be the givers and not the takers. Lastly, love is a powerful force that doesn't bloom in a field of pride and selfishness. How many of the wise and learned and others understand this? I am sad to say, it took me a very long time.

So, how does the Spirit world set us up to learn and to grow into responsible and respectful humans?

## Forgetfulness of the Past - Why?

When we reincarnate, we are not allowed to remember our past lives or our time as a spirit. To determine why this is so, let's examine a case of a spirit who was reincarnated with the ability to remember past lives. In the book, *The Messengers*, psychographed by Francisco C. Xavier, dictated to him by the spirit Andre Luiz, Andre encounters a person who completely failed in his mission on earth. Joel, the spirit who laments his failure, tells Andre;

> "My failure was not because of too much sensitivity, but because of how I used it. As I understand now, God allows some individuals to have superior sensitivity so they can use it as a tool, a kind of powerful magnifying lens that helps them see the right course of life for themselves and others they are supposed to help. This extra sensitivity can help to perceive life's path, identify dangers and shortcuts, and clearly see obstacles. Instead of using the gift in that way, all I did was use it to satisfy my warped curiosity about myself."

> "To fulfill my role of helping others, my expanded perception included the ability to remember my past lives. Most people can't recall their own past, and for good reason. In my case, I was supposed to use that knowledge in my service to help others, not to obsess about it, and that's where I failed."

> "I began to obsess about a previous existence in which I has been Monsignor Alejandre Pizarro who participated in the last years of the cruel Spanish Inquisition. That's when I started misusing the spiritual magnifying lens I told you about. The excitement of the sensations was inebriating – it was as if I was addicted to drugs or alcohol – and I neglected all of my previously accepted responsibilities."

"I started spending all of my time trying to locate the people who had been my companions during my time centuries before as a religious man. I forced myself to find each and every one of them in space and time, reconstituting their biographical sketches, completely ignoring the work I was supposed to do."[27]

"So I spent my life in this fashion – going from revelation to revelation, sensation to sensation. I, who had reincarnated with the unusual ability to remember in order to be useful transformed my gift into a tool of addiction. I'd thrown away an opportunity to redeem myself, and I lived tortured by intermittent bouts of hallucination. The misuse of my sensitivity generated an imbalance in my mind so that I became painfully unstable."[28]

A perfect example of what could happen when we know too much and are unable to focus on what we need to learn. Imagine sitting in a classroom, with the TV blaring, showing you scenes from your previous existence while you attempt to comprehend the basic facts of Algebra. One could not possibly possess the mental force to concentrate on that valuable lesson, especially if you had had some type of mathematics background before and tried to merge it with what you are learning at the present time. Not only would you reject parts of what were offered to you, but you would be exasperated with having to sit through this lecture again, even though spaced out by hundreds of years.

There are other reasons as well. In *The Gospel According to Spiritism*, it says, "A spirit is frequently reborn into the same environment in which it has already lived and finds itself in relationships with the same individuals in order to repair the wrong it did to them. If it were to recognize in them those whom it used to hate, perhaps its hatred would reawaken. In any case, it would feel humiliated in the presence of those it offended."[29] Therefore, the need to forget the past, not only that of our present life but from previous lives as well is a necessity to be able to learn and to forgive others and to grow spiritually.

That said, are we a completely blank slate, always starting

over? No, for again in *The Gospel According to Spiritism*, we are told, "God has given us for our advancement precisely what is necessary and what will be enough for us: the voice of conscience and our instinctive tendencies, taking from us what could harm us."[30] The underlines are mine. These are the two main levers of our behavior. If our conscience (or instinct) tells us something is wrong, I suggest that such warnings come with the wisdom of hundreds, if not thousands, of years of experience behind them.

## Why We Must Endure Childhood?

Traveling through childhood is a vital part of our learning process. The importance of this is explained in *The Spirits Book*;

> *383. What is, the use, for a spirit, of passing through the state of infancy?*
>
> "The aim of incarnation is the improvement of the spirit subjected to it; and a spirit is more accessible during childhood to the impressions he receives, and which may conduce to his advancement – the end to which all those who are entrusted with his education should contribute."[31]

Therefore, while we are young, we have the opportunity to change our basic dispositions and instincts for the better, since we are in a more open and trusting state. Hopefully, this will allow us to improve our performance in later life and help us to attain a higher awareness of spirituality. This point is reinforced by the following statement later in *The Spirits Book*, "The weakness of corporeal youth tends to render them more pliable, more amenable to the counsels of those whose experience should aid their progress. It is thus that evil tendencies are repressed, and faulty characters are gradually reformed."[32] What more does one need to fully understand the significance of being good parents? Our first mission here on earth is to create a loving and enriching atmosphere for our children. It is our duty to supply the structure, morally and physically, to give our children the best chances possible for a successful life.

But why do we sometimes see examples of horrible parents?

Why does God allow this? *The Spirits Book* supplies the answer:

> *891. Since maternal affection is a natural sentiment, why is it that mothers often hate their children, and even, in some cases, before their birth?*
>
> "The absence of maternal affection is sometimes a trial chosen by the spirit of the child, or an expiation for him if he has been a bad father, bad mother, or a bad son, in some previous existence. In all cases, a bad mother can only be the incarnation of a bad spirit, who seeks to throw obstacles in the path of the child, in order to make him succumb in the trial he has chosen. But such a violation of the laws of nature will not remain unpunished, and the spirit of the child will be rewarded for surmounting the obstacles thus thrown in his way."[33]

## When does the Phase of Childhood Innocence End?

When do the instinctive tendencies and the conscience of the spirit start to reveal themselves and make the child less pliable? The answer is slightly variable, as shown by this passage in *The Spirits Book*, about when a child starts to be more influenced by it past experiences, "But, when children no longer need this protection, this assistance, which has been given them during fifteen or twenty years, their real character and individuality reappears in all of its nudity. He who is really good remains good; but, even then, his character reveals many traits and shades that were hidden during his earlier years."[34]

Therefore, it is not just teenage rebellion that is occurring, but a reawakening of a person's true character. If the parents are successful in their molding of the child, even a relatively less advanced spirit will benefit from those formative years. A Good spirits will take the learning given to them and build upon it.

## What Happens When a Child Dies?

Some religions which profess the existence of reincarnation believe that when a child dies, the spirit returns to an adult form, so they may start over. In a few of the books by Andre Luiz, there are mentions of places where spirits care for children. One would think this would be a rare occurrence; after all newly formed spirits are first reincarnated upon primitive worlds. There is an explanation to this mystery in the book *Between Heaven and Earth,* by Francisco C. Xavier, inspired by the spirit Andre Luiz. Andre Luiz is talking to his companions when they are visiting a center for spirit children and as usual Andre is curious about such centers, he records the following conversation;

> "According to the old, classical theology, newborns remained in limbo after death, without the glory of heaven or the torment of hell, whereas of late, with the new concepts of spiritualism, such discarnates have been thought to immediately resume their adult personage."
>
> "A lot of times that is what actually happens." explains Blandina. "When the spirit has reached an elevated evolutionary level and has assumed mental command of itself, it acquires the ability to easily disengage itself from the imposition of the physical form, overcoming the difficulties of pre-adult discarnation. We know of great souls who were reborn for a very short time, simply with the objective of awakening beloved hearts to the acquisition of moral values. Then, right afterwards, they recover their former appearance. However, the same does not apply for most children that discarnate. Souls that are still prisoners of unconscious automatism are relatively a long way from self- governance. They rest and are led by nature, like babies in their mothers' laps. They are unable to undo the ties that bind them to the rigid principles that guide the world of forms: thus, they need time in order to be renewed. That is why we cannot do without the recovery time needed for someone who has left the physical vehicle in infancy, because after the biological struggle of reincarnation or discarnation for those who are in the early stages of acquiring mental power, time has to function as an indispensable element for restoration. The length of that time depends on how the learner applies him or herself to acquire inner light through his or her own moral growth."[35]

Hence, once again, our ability to free ourselves from the materialistic world and concentrate on loving and helping others does make a difference in subsequent lives. With a superior pool of knowledge we are able to recover our spiritual form, while those who have been reincarnated to begin another trial without first attaining a taste of the wonderfulness of spiritual life are at a disadvantage. We truly are creatures of our own mind. We should invest as much energy in the development of our inner bodies as we do in our outward appearance.

# Chapter 6 – How You Map Out Your Trials on Earth

I am sure you have read or heard before that we are on earth to learn. Essentially, we are in a classroom, learning by doing, absorbing new ideas and attitudes by experiences. Did you also know that, most probably, you are the one that selected your intended course work? So, when things get tough, you have no one to blame but yourself!

We live our lives believing that we exist in the realm of chance. Somehow, our parents conceived us, we grew up and went to school in some particular location, not of our choosing but by chance. It was a place where our parents decided to live at the time, another decision mandated by random occurrences. We go to college or into a profession by some whim, or happenstance, such as an uncle knowing a person who knows a person. We strive and learn through our early adulthood; sometimes we succeed and other times we fail miserably. We curse the events that led us to despair. Somehow, we survive, and at each step we gather small morsels of wisdom along the way. We detest the lessons we had to learn, but nevertheless, in our hearts, we recognize the value of our accumulated knowledge.

But what if, and just think about this for a moment, what if all of this was planned? No, not down to the last detail, but the broad strokes. The major and not so major events of your life, pre-ordained. And not prearranged by some distant entity, but by you. Yes, you are the one who is responsible for this mess! This life of yours. Both the good and the bad.

## Reason for Reincarnation

Let's start at the beginning. In The Spirits Book, Allan Kardec codified the answer as to why we must reincarnate:

*132. What is the aim of the incarnation of spirits?*

"It is a necessity imposed on them by God, as the means of

attaining perfection. For some of them it is an expiation; for others, a mission. In order to attain perfection, it is necessary for them to undergo all the vicissitudes of corporeal existence. It is the experience acquired by expiation that constitutes its usefulness. Incarnation has also another aim, namely, that of fitting the spirit to perform his share in the work of creation; for which purpose he is made to assume a corporeal apparatus in harmony with the material state of each world into which he is sent, and by means of which he is enabled to accomplish the special work, in connection with that world which has been appointed to him by the divine ordering. He is thus made to contribute his quota towards the general weal, while achieving his own advancement. "[36]

## Planning for the New Life

In the book *Memoirs of a Suicide*, psychographed by Yvonne Pereira, a group of spirits are told about the planning of a new life, by a veteran of reincarnation planning;

> "The planning of the events relating to a reincarnation will be rigorously studied, firmed up, and revised, always in accordance with utmost justice … in fulfillment of the highest expression of the immortal decree sanction by the Divine Master – which explains all the problems that afflict and bound Humanity:
>
> "*To each according to his deeds*."[37]

Hence, our plans begin with what we must correct from a previous life and what we wish to learn in our next life. It is as if we are in High School, looking through all of the college catalogs that have finally arrived, attempting to ascertain what our future will be. The basic conditions of planning are explained;

> "Normally, candidates for reincarnation choose their own trials, the acres of thorns that will dilacerate the days of their earthly lives, and where they will get the chance to amend the consequences of their guilty past. They themselves will beseech the Guiding Powers for new opportunities that will

enable them to demonstrate their repentance and their desire to enter a redemptive path that will offer them the chance to correct the inferior impulses that drove them to their wrongful conduct ... These trials can be experienced in a relatively sound body if the mental suffering is extreme, or in a deformed body, or in one stricken by an incurable disease. It all depends on the extent of the offense and the demerits involved.

So, the patients themselves actually sketch out the charts for their future physical body and the plan for the principal and unavoidable events they must undergo, the logical and inseparable effects of the causes created by their infractions; but they are always assisted by their dedicated mentors."[38]

The lecture above was given to suicides, which is why the choice of a sound body, with more experiences for learning than trials for payment was not covered. However, the concept remains, we ourselves will direct the trials and the type of physical covering we shall inhabit for our next life, Therefore, you yourself likely elected the body you are in, while you are reading this article, with the exact eyes you chose.

## Planning for your Body

Choosing your physical body is more difficult that it seems. You know that imperfect nose of yours? Well, you determined not to have the latest fashion in noses. How do we know that? In the book, *Missionaries of the Light*, psychographed by Francisco C. Xavier, inspired by the spirit Andre Luiz, a woman who is actively planning her trials for the next life, talks about her reasoning;

"'I have been advised by benefactors here that I should avoid re-entering earth with flawless body lines. If I do avoid it, I might have a better success in the tasks I'm planning; I would be grateful if the thyroid and the parathyroid glands were not so perfectly outlined. As you know, my task will not be easy. I need to recapture a large spiritual heritage. I must avoid any possibility of failure and perfect physical harmony would get in the way of my goals.'

My new companion gave me an expressive look and said to her:

'You're right. Physical seductiveness is a real danger, not only for those who radiate its influence but also for those who are subject to it.'

'I would prefer an unattractive body,' she replied. 'I'm not interested in a body like Venus; I'm interested in the redemption of my spirit for eternity.'"[39]

Therefore, those of you who don't care for your body, think hard about what other matters you should be concentrating on, rather than focusing on your vanity. You picked the model you are in for a reason.

One would also ask, what about the DNA we inherit from our parents? Doesn't that lay the foundation of our form? Andre Luiz asked the same question;

"What about the law of physiological heredity?" Andre Luiz asked.

His mentor answered:

"It works with inalienable control upon all evolving beings, but of course it is subject to the influence of those who attain qualities that are superior to the general environment. Furthermore, when individuals interested in new experiences in the physical realm are deserving of 'intercessory' services, the higher powers can impress certain modifications on matter from the embryological development onward if they determine that alterations are needed for the work of redemption."[40]

Therefore, we must start with what our parents offer; next our own perispirit (that part of us which envelops our intended body) will affect our germination while in the womb. Lastly, the spirit world is able to perform minute surgery on our DNA to alter our appearance and innate abilities.

Not only do we determine the complete diagram of our bodies, but we also plan in advance afflictions that await us. Andre talks to a spirit who works in the Reincarnation Planning Center in the heavenly city Nosso Lar. He points out the extent of our future planning:

> "Here is the plan for the future reincarnation of a friend of mine. Do you see some dark spots from the descending colon to the sigmoid loop? This indicates that he will suffer from a large ulcer in this area as soon as he becomes an adult. Nevertheless, he has chosen it."[41]

Now, I wonder why I had my kidney stones! What exquisite torture! What in the heck did I do to warrant that experience? It must have been wicked and I most certainly deserved it, but I wish I knew, so I could take some satisfaction from learning my lesson with my pain. But I tell you this, whatever I did, I won't do it again!

### Planning for your Trials

Our body is but one consideration for our next life. We must also plan the trials, the events that push us forward in our exploration of knowledge. There is an example of a suicide, in the book, *Memoirs of a Suicide*, Jeronimo, who defrauded his business associates, lost all of his money and fled the situation he created by taking his own life. He left behind a wife, a son, and three daughters, all left destitute. Jeronimo tells his friends about his plans for his next life;

> "I won't be able to have children! By not looking after my family; by rejecting, half way through, the honorable responsibility of being head of the household in order to help me ascend in merit. I put myself in the wretched position of not being granted the chance of building a family and being a father again in my next existence!"

> "However, in order to mitigate my ugly behavior toward Zulmira and my children, I have promised Mother Mary, the sublime mother of my Redeemer, whose maternal solicitude rehabilitated Margarida and Albino, to employ all my efforts to

assist orphaned children, to somehow build shelters for them and to become their guardian, as if they were my own!"[42]

Jeronimo has planned his family life to compensate for what he did in his previous life. He has also planned his financial status in his next life. His friends express happiness in his helping orphans, but they are worried if he will have the financial resources to follow through. He informs them, that at first he will be rich, born into a wealthy family. Next he says; "May Heaven allow it, indeed my friend! ... Because before or after the financial ruin that awaits me during my expiatory existence, I shall have become the supporter of many, many orphans."[43]

Notice, how for each of his major failings, he will have to redeem himself in one way or another. Once again, he shall recognize the despair of bankruptcy and the complete withdraw of all of his old friends. He shall deeply feel the pull of suicide, but if he wishes to be victorious in his new life, he will have to resist that urge with all of his facilities.

Our life is laid out in great detail. We don't have the freedom to not participate in our trials; our freedom lies in our response to events. Therefore, it is better to attack life with the attitude of a child, with an open mind and an acceptance of all that occurs. It behooves us to learn from each hurdle, gain wisdom and internalize how this understanding will carry us through multiple lives as we ascend as a spirit.

# Chapter 7 – Why We Must Go Through Multiple Trials

Reincarnation is an accepted process for Spiritists. The need to atone for your wrongs in the next life is well known. But there are other reasons for re-birth as well. The spirit Andre Luiz delves deeper into the need for varied experiences and sheds light on the complexities in our learning here on earth in two of his books, *Missionaries of the Light* and *Workers of the Life Eternal*, both psychographed by Francisco C. Xavier.

To understand the need for multiple lives, even for those whose rays of goodness made an impact on earth in their previous existence, we need to understand why even the best of us must return to earth to complete our studies. The most common perception for the need for each successive life is the requirement to pay off our debts incurred in our previous life. The next thought that comes to us is the need to perform good deeds and be a positive influence for those around us. While all of this is true, there are more complex reasons at work.

The great Brazilian medium, Francisco C. Xavier, who publish more than 400 books in his life time, psychographed a series of books dictated by a spirit of a deceased Brazilian doctor named Andre Luiz. Using Francisco C. Xavier (known as Chico Xavier), Andre Luiz dictated these books so that we here on earth could understand what goes on in the Spirit world.

Andre Luiz's first book, *Nosso Lar*, is the story of his death and about his wandering in the place between "heaven" and "hell", as a result of his actions during his most recent incarnation. Eventually he was rescued by good spirits who took him to a heavenly city named Nosso Lar. He was tasked by the spirit world to assist various teams of spirits, and could relay to us the different types and methods of work that exist in the spirit life after physical death. Many of his books have been translated into English, and *Nosso Lar* has been made into a movie, with English subtitles. The movie title in English is "Astral City: A Spiritual Journey".

In the book, *Missionaries of the Light*, Andre Luiz narrates his experience inside the Design and Planning Pavilions of Nosso Lar, where spirits draw up plans for uncommon reincarnations, there he hears the term "completer". Curious he asks his friend Silverio, who kindly explains:

> "It is the title that applies to those rare brothers and sisters who profited from all the constructive potential that their earthly body offered them. Generally, in returning to the physical realm, almost all of us miss significant opportunities while wasting our physiological energies. We wander around, doing something useful for ourselves and for others, but sometimes we waste fifty, sixty, seventy percent, and often even more, of our potential. On many occasions, we also have the aggravating circumstance of having used the sacred energies of life on unworthy activities that degrade our mind and harden our heart. However, those who use their physical machine as faithful workers will acquire significant rights in our realm. As loyal and productive workers, 'completers' are free to choose their future body when they return to the earth on missions of love and enlightenment, or they may receive an ennobled physical vessel for the continuation of their tasks on their way to higher circles of work."[44]

When Silverio uses the term 'rare', he is doing so in the context of those spirits who are elevated enough to earn and use the full capabilities of the Design and Planning Pavilions. Why would these individuals fail to fully profit from the gifts given to them? To comprehend this, Andre wishes to understand the type of person who is receiving preparations for his or her next life and the services provided in the Design and Planning Pavilion.

## Design and Planning Pavilion

Andre learns that the Design and Planning Pavilion not only creates the blueprints for the physical body of a reincarnate, but also plans for its future weaknesses. Andre's guide at the Pavilion, Manasses, shows a diagram of a future reincarnation and points out, "Here is the plan for the future reincarnation of a friend of mine. Do you see some dark spots from the descending colon to the sigmoid loop? This indicates that he will suffer from a large ulcer in this area as soon as he becomes an adult."[45] Andre is told that this person had stabbed another over one hundred years ago. He had made amends in the spirit world with his victim and had accomplished many good deeds; nevertheless he requested that he pay for his debt. The requirement that all debts be fully paid is a recurring theme in the Spiritist world. Until the person who committed the deed feels he or she has paid full restitution, even when others would consider them fully paid off, that person will not feel exonerated from the crime. We are our own harshest judges of our conduct.

Andre also wished to know if his friend knew if any of the 'completers' have returned to earth and if they returned with perfect bodies? He was told, "Despite their merit, none of those whom I have seen leave chose flawless forms. They requested arrangements for a healthy existence, more concerned with the resistance, balance, durability and strength of the instrument that was to serve them. But they also asked for measures that would temporarily decrease their personal magnetism, avoiding a highly beautiful physical appearance and thereby concealing the beauty of their souls in order to guarantee the effectiveness of their tasks."[46]

Given their past successes and track records of achievement, one would think the spirits classified as 'completers' would have the capability to achieve their goals in any environment. Andre listens to the explanation, "They did this because, living under the rules of appearances when on earth, most people, if they were aware of their true status, would try to crush such missionaries of the good by means of the destructive vibrations of jealousy, spite, gratuitous antipathy and unwarranted quarrels."[47]

Therefore, not only do we need to learn how to fulfill our missions, but we must also acquire the methods to deal with success, in terms of physical beauty, intelligence, charisma, as well as also how to deal with the consequences of our presence in the minds of others. The very fact that we merely exist on earth, without any action on our part, comes with a host of difficult lessons to learn.

## The Need for Balance

Andre Luiz was assigned to a group of spirits who assisted people leaving their earthly life in the book, *Workers of the Life Eternal*, where he underwent multiple experiences at people's bedsides and witnessed the dramas that swirled around them. He weighs the numerous scenes and stories of people struggling to depart and comes to the conclusion:

> "Studying cases of death had enriched my knowledge in the field of mental science. The spirit (eternal in essence) makes use of matter (transitory in its associations) as didactic material that evolves more and more in the spirit's never ending course of experience toward integration within the Supreme Divinity."[48]

What does Andre mean by didactic material in this instance? One of the definitions of didactic is "teaching or intended to teach a moral lesson."[49] Therefore as we continue learning in the spirit world and travel through multiple physical trials on earth we accumulate moral lessons that in turn influence our physical bodies and the structure of our brain, as we are reborn. Not only is our intellectual being as spirits is important, but the physical makeup of our human form is vital for both our present involvement on our planet and to our eventual elevation as spirits.

Andre continues to explain his thesis stating, "When we harm matter, we will in turn have complicated the service schedule that is so vital to our spiritual progress, and in any situation we will remain at a standstill in order to restore the sublime heritage that has been placed at our disposal by the Imperishable Goodness."[50]

Andre is pointing out that destroying our bodies or minds, by such acts of excessive drinking or by a criminal action, delays and would subtract from our accumulating the correct amount of learning to move up in our spiritual plane.

Andre goes on further to detail the penalty of such actions, "We will be compelled to regenerative work both during incarnation and discarnation, both in our corporeal existence and in the death of our body, both in the present and in the future. No one will successfully reach the peak of life eternal without first having learned the balance to do so."[51] He observed, after personally seeing the end of life experiences of multiple people, the passion to hold onto material objects, the regrets of wrong doing, the terrible physical inflictions caused by alcoholism or drugs, the totality of the effect on the spirit as it withdraws from the body.

On the other hand, spirits who led a life relatively free from such actions, achieved a calmer death, a faster withdrawal from their bodies. The spirits who did not resist temptation experienced a much harder effort to let go. Even after full withdraw of their spirits from their physical bodies, these types of people were confused and required intensive care to fully recover their thought processes.

Given all that he had seen, Andre fully realizes the need for our multiple attempts at learning in our corporeal bodies and "hence the reasons for the complex activities of the evolutionary road, the countless diversities, the multiplicity of social positions, the degrees of abilities and the levels of intelligence on the various planes of life."[52] What a wonderful revelation! We all go through periods of high social positions, living life with riches, and being the smartest person in the room. Meanwhile, we also live in the opposite positions. Truly, this knowledge must inspire us all to be humble.

For those who believe we only need one life to be pure, it is as if we wanted to be the president of a large company without ever working any other job. Of course we must start in the mail room and work our way up in various positions to fully comprehend how things get done and how to survive within the culture of the organization. No matter how pious we could have started out as a new spirit, we would still need the required know-how to gain our elevation. Only through rigorous trials do we have the right mixture of beliefs and knowledge to reincarnate with good prospects of success and to serve as valued worker in the spirit realm.

When the balance of experience is lacking, we are less able to control the process of reincarnation and control ourselves in a physical form. Hence, the problems we may have at times with periods of depression, caused by the inability to stabilize ourselves, because we lack the required combination of experiences to be able to mold our thoughts in the correct manner for all situations. This frustration of controlling ourselves and trying to learn how to cope with life is familiar to any teenager. We did not know that this is a multiple-lives-long task. Be content, even later in life as we live within the ups and downs, that we are gaining valuable training, which will carry over to the next life in subtle ways.

# Chapter 8 – Interlude 1 – The Past Lives of Camilo Castelo Branco

The fact that we reincarnate means that all of us has had past lives. Therefore, to understand the reasons we reincarnate in different situations, it is beneficial to analyze the past lives of others, so we may determine why some people have the arc of lifes that were given to them. One such fascinating subject is Camilo Branco, who was a famous Portuguese author who lived in Portugal in the 19th century. He committed suicide in 1890. Communicating with the medium Yvonne Pereira, Camilo told his story. Part of his narrative is the history of his past lives. Camilo was one of the hecklers as Jesus struggled by, carrying the cross, on the way to be crucified.

Camilo Castelo Branco wasn't just an ordinary suicide. He was a commanding figure in Portugal's literary scene in the late 1800's. He was known as the Portuguese Balzac and was awarded the title of Viscount of Correia Botelho. In despair over his son's insanity and his own ailments that would certainly lead to blindness, he ended his life in 1890.[53]

According to his Wikipedia page, "Camilo produced over 260 works, ranging from essays, plays, romantic fiction to non-fiction. His writing is considered original in that it combines the dramatic and sentimental spirit of Romanticism with a highly personal combination of sarcasm, bitterness and dark humor. He is also celebrated for his peculiar wit and anecdotal character, as well as for his turbulent (and ultimately tragic) life."[54]

Ordinarily, this is where his story would end. Camilo would live in our memories only for as long as his books didn't naturally deteriorate, or if the internet failed to archive his life but in some remote corner, where only the most dedicated researcher would discover any mention of him.

However, Camilo inspired the medium Yvonne A. Pereira to write about his life after physical death, his after-life biography. In the book, *Memoirs of a Suicide*, we are taken from the moment Camilo kills himself to years later to when he is preparing to re-enter our physical world to subject himself to the required trials to pay for his wrongs and to learn the lessons so he may improve his immortal spirit.

The first paragraph of the book takes you to the place reserved for suicides:

> "It was the month of January, 1891, when I found myself being held in an area of the Invisible World. Its desolate landscape was comprised of deep valleys that were continuously enveloped in shadowy darkness. Within its winding gorges and sinister caves, spirits that used to be men and women on the earth howled like hordes of infuriated demons, demented by the absolutely unconceivable intensity and strangeness of the sufferings that tormented them."[55]

Only when his natural years of living ended is Camilo taken out of that horrid landscape and up to the "Mary of Nazareth" Hospital. The latter is a spirit colony reserved for suicides, men and women, to recuperate after their ordeal and to learn about their obligations to their sacred mission to fully live out the life they had chosen beforehand. Running in cowardice from one's assigned tribulations in the physical life results in severe penalties. As part of his rehabilitation, Camilo must learn what brought him to his decision to escape his ailments and why he was given the sufferings that he should have endured with dignity.

## Past Life – 33 A.D.

For Camilo to understand why he was destined to be blind in old age, he needed to have his past wrongs exposed. As there is a reason for everything that happens to us, our lives are finely orchestrated to test and uplift us, as well as hammer out, with our head upon an anvil, the bad habits and intentions that we have carried for too long.

As part of his preparation for a fruitful return to a physical body, he was taken to a classroom amphitheater where he is strapped into a device that would take him back to his past. This is not merely witnessing a picture on a screen, but a complete four dimensional experience, where he and his fellow classmates were inside his preceding lives. He was nervous, for all of the previous students had revealed crimes and failures to be ashamed of for several lifetimes. The narrative begins:

> "I went back to the year 33 A.D! However, I was not only remembering it: I was actually living in that time period, exactly as before!
>
> The old holy city of the Jews – Jerusalem – was experiencing feverish events on that hot, sunny morning. I felt possessed by a diabolical happiness as I walked through the streets packed with foreigners, inciting riots, encouraging fights, spreading disquieting gossip, promoting disorder. It was the feast day of Calvary, and it was known that a certain revolutionary named Jesus of Nazareth had been condemned by the authorities of Rome to die on the cross, along with two other criminals."[56]

Camilo knew he was "a wretched person, poor and evil."[57] He lived off of the discarded clothes and food of others. His greatest pleasure was to witness misfortune, of any kind, drunks, fights and torture. He found himself following Jesus, so he can witness pain and suffering:

> "Fierce in my obstinacy, I follow him on his dolorous climb, yelling offenses and vile scorn; and I must confess that the only reason I do not strike him with stones with the violence of my murderous arm is because he is so closely guarded by the Roman soldiers. The truth is that I have always felt myself to be inferior and belittled everywhere I go. I feel envy and hatred towards everything that actually is, or that I believe to be, superior to me! Ugly, disheveled, ignoble, deformed – I had only one arm – degraded, ambitious, the stuff of pure evil dripped from my heart."[58]

Wait, it gets worse. He noticed Mary, the mother of Jesus, and yelled out insults and sarcastic remarks to her. Anything to hurt everyone around him. A man with one arm, for what offense he lost an arm, we will never know, but he was on a mission to equally harm the world. A man who was rescued from the valley of the suicides by the very woman he abused more than 1800 years earlier.

I can't imagine the nightmare of discovering his deeds. I can only contemplate in fear what horrible crimes I must have committed in some previous wretched life, for all of us are on the path to become better, which means that in the past we have made choice that we would scorn and disapprove of today.

After witnessing the death of Christ, Camilo went on to take part in the stoning of Stephen. He readily assisted the Sanhedrin to ferret out Christians. Then he discovered:

> "In fact, I was not even a son of Israel! I had come from far away, an adventurer and disbeliever, from distant Gaul. I had fled my own tribe, where I had been condemned to death for the double crime of murder and treason to my homeland, having arrived in Judea by chance in the last months of the Lord's ministry."[59]

His life during the time of Christ was one of constant strife, caused by his own defective character. He did not experience any redeeming act while reliving his nightmare of impiety.

## Past Life – 17th Century - Spain

Camilo next experienced life after life, centuries of trials, always as a base person, without moral guidance. His only wish was to gain wealth and pleasure. Sometimes he would climb high on the social ladder, but the expected improvement in his spiritual state never materialized. Hence, whenever he climbed high, he fell further each time his wrongs were discovered. His lives were always located in the regions of France or Spain.

In between lives, he would learn about the spiritual principles that would be presented to the world in the form of the Doctrine of Spiritism in the 1850s. Camilo desired the progression of the state of his soul. He knew that he should learn how to be charitable, loving, unselfish and fraternal. But his motivations for adapting these attributes were in the expectation that he could use them to "appear" good, while accumulating more riches and other advantages all for his use.

Finally, in the early seventeenth century, he found himself in a confused state in a dark dungeon. Slowly the fog lifted and his life became apparent:

> "I was born into an old family of bankrupt nobles, who, at the time, were besieged by insurmountable adversities, such as political and religious rivalries, as well as disagreements with the Crown.
>
> In my early youth I was illiterate, fraught by hard toil in the fields. I tended sheep and tilled the soil like a wretched serf, dividing myself amongst multiple tasks under the severe eye of my father, a cruel, provincial nobleman, whose unrestrained religious pride, inspired by the ideas of the Reformation, has disgraced him before the king."[60]

Born in Toledo, Spain in adverse conditions, but still with prospects because of his noble birth, Camilo was once again provided a chance to rise above his past. Ambitious, even at his young age, Camilo was able to enlist the aid of the parish priest to educate him. As he grew older he became fixated on the idea of marriage and surveyed the women in his circle of acquaintances. He focused on his mother's niece:

> "Her name was Maria Magda. She was slender and beautiful, and had black, fragrant, waist-length, braided hair, along with languid and seductive eyes. Like me, she was the daughter of bankrupt nobles, but thanks to her parents' thoughtfulness, she had the advantage of having acquired a good domestic and social education."[61]

When a more prosperous rival appeared, Camilo was left alone and bitter. As his past character would react, so would his present, in the deepest part of his mind, he thirsted for revenge. He showed no hint of understanding that Maria may have loved another or that the wishes of her parents influenced her decision; just a primitive urge to strike back at the cause of his pain. Hence, he swore eternal revenge against his love, Maria, and her new husband, Jacinto de Ornelas.

From then on, he eliminated the thought of marriage from his mind and concentrated his immense energy on the means to better his station. He thus pursued a social plateau where he could enjoy power over the objects of his scorn, supremacy enough to humiliate and destroy the unsuspecting couple.

The spirit world attempted to guide Camilo back onto the path of self-improvement:

> "I dreamed night after night that my old father, as well as other deceased friends, had returned from the grave to advise me to give up on my plans for the future; instead, I should marry one of my childhood friends, a decision that would be the surest path to peace-of-mind and true happiness."[62]

The spirit world does not want us to fail. We are watched with the loving kindness of a true mother and father. Their affection rains down upon us. This is why we have a conscience. Although we temporarily lose the conscious recollection of our memories from past lives when we are reborn, we retain two vital signal posts. The first is our conscience; our accumulated moral learning from all of our past lives serves to govern us in our daily decisions. When we reflect on an action, our conscience provides us feedback. We must listen to that advice and heed it for within us we have centuries of stored wisdom.

Our instincts are the second guiderail that has been betrothed to us in our current life. Multiple life experiences in countless sets of circumstances have toned our instincts, whereby we are given the gift to recognize the potentially adverse *or* positive significance of any situation.

The death of his father allowed Camilo to discover his road to revenge. He joined the Society of Jesus, where he received a sterling education. Ignoring the company of truly dedicated servants of Jesus within the ranks, he sought out those whose favor could raise him up in the organization. Meanwhile the Jesuits, representing the spearhead of the infamous Spanish Inquisition, welcomed young lieutenants who did not hesitate to arrest innocents, partake in slander and torture victims when ordered. He describes his fanaticism:

> "I would have turned in my own father; such was the madness that took hold of me. I would have dragged him before the tribunal as an agent of the Reformation if he had not surrendered his soul to the Creator, thanks to the mercy of Heaven! However, I did not do all of that to give vent to my own evilness: my intent was only to serve my superiors, to exalt the Jesuit cause, to prove the unending dedication and unconditional gratitude my passionate soul could muster for all the support they had given me! I myself became a victim of that very institution, because in recognizing my submission for the favors I had received, my superiors took advantage of my sentiments and induced me to commit abominable crimes, certain as they were that I would be incapable of betrayal."[63]

Camilo worked his way up among the ranks of the Jesuits for fifteen years, until, one day, he discovered that the husband of his love, Maria had returned from duty in Holland. Jacinto had arrived back in Spain with great honors. Camilo sent his spies to watch every movement of the couple. Maria and Jacinto had a good marriage with children. They were very much in love and Maria was known for her impeccable virtues.

Trying to worm his way into a renewal of passion with Maria, he met her at the church she visited every week. Then he started to frequent her house. He praised, flattered and implored her for affection. She resisted at every turn. Even her husband noticed his intentions, but against a member of the dreaded Spanish Inquisition, he was powerless to stop Camilo's advances. Besides, Jacinto knew his leanings toward the Reformation he witnessed in Holland could be a lever to destroy his life and forever affect the lives of his children.

Jacinto prepared to leave Madrid for safety, but Camilo found out and he turned Jacinto over to the authorities, on suspicion of being a Huguenot (a member of the French protestant reformed church). Camilo successfully fabricated evidence to convict Jacinto and requested that Jacinto be handed over to him. Jacinto's tortures by Camilo are recorded thusly:

> "I had his fingernails and teeth yanked out; his fingers and wrists disjointed; the soles of his feet slowly, patiently burned with red-hot blades. I had him flogged until his flesh shredded, and all of it under the pretext of saving him from hell, for having apostatized, forcing him to make confessions of supposed conspiracies against the Church, under whose name I took shelter for such vile acts."[64]

Knowing the cause of her husband's incarceration, Maria went to plead with Camilo to release her husband. Camilo forced Maria to give in to all of his wishes. While Maria did all that Camilo demanded, he could see the disdain in her eyes. Therefore, tiring of his malicious game, he decided to return her husband to her. However, Camilo had one more horrible deed to accomplish:

> "Maria had pleaded for the life and freedom of her husband and I had promised to concede them. But she had forgotten to ask me to return him intact, without mutilations! Therefore, *I had his eyes gouged out with a red-hot iron, thus barbarically disfiguring him, forever plunging him into the darkness of indescribable torment.* I never even dreamed that there was an Almighty God following from the height of his Justice my abominable act, which I archived in the folds of my conscience as if reflected in a mirror in order to accuse me and demand unappealable atonement throughout the centuries!"[65]

Two months after being released, Jacinto, using a knife he asked his five-year-old son to fetch him, committed suicide. Finally realizing the extent of his crimes, Camilo could not sleep. He suffered from incessant nightmares and could no longer carry out the orders of his superiors. Subsequently, falling out of favor, he was imprisoned for life by the same institution that he had been so dedicated in carrying out their diabolical commands. He died alone in his cell, full of regrets.

At this point in his spiritual interrogation, Camilo finally realized why he was destined for blindness in his last life. He knew that he was meant to face the same dread and hopelessness that his innocent victim felt three hundred years earlier. Even worse was that he didn't have the courage to face it; instead he weakened and sought to immediately escape his intended misfortune.

Camilo now understood that it wasn't divine providence that determined that he was to be blind in his old age, but himself. His actions had consequences, and between physical lives, he determined the trials and the lessons he should live through. He leaves us with this thought:

> "The truth is that it was a situation of my own creation, caused by my own wrongs and defects down through the ages!"[66]

Past lives are important for us. Even though we may not recall, while incarnated, what they were, we can, by analyzing the trials, obstacles, and events of our present life, infer what we must repair and learn in this life. We must never be deterred in finishing our assigned task. The harsher our trials, the more we have to learn from them, and we should be grateful for the opportunity to recover our moral debts and resume stepping up the ladder of purification of our souls.

# Chapter 9 – Why are Some Burdened with Disabilities

Seeing poor souls in deformed bodies, or those with other types of severe disabilities is one of the main reasons why many people question the existence and /or justice of God. They ask "How could God be so cruel?" According to Divine Law, spirits are required to go through such trials when the choices made in their past warrant them. In the last chapter we discovered the life of Camilo Branco and saw how his cruelty in previous lives affected his trials in his next life. Now we shall go more in depth about what could be the consequences of our actions.

Yvonne A. Pereira psychographed the book *Memoirs of a Suicide*, published in 1955, with the help of two spirits. The first is Camilo Candido Botelho (his real name is Camilo Castelo Branco), the Portuguese writer whose story we recounted in the previous chapter. The other spirit is Leon Denis, who was one of the leading apostles of Spiritism after the passing of Allan Kardec[67].

The spirit author, Camilo spent some time in the lower zones, a very unpleasant episode, and when his intended life span completed, he was picked up and taken to the Mary of Nazareth Hospital. The entire complex was controlled by the mother of Jesus and was dedicated to suicides. Camilo endured a lengthy process to recover from his desperate act. As part of his recovery he and the group he was recovering with, were able to speak with knowledgeable spirits about the various aspects of the Spirit Hospital complex in which they spent their recovery. One of the areas of the Hospital contained the spirits who still lived in a stupor, unable to function in the spirit world. Camilo was told about this pitiful group:

> "Be on the lookout for this new sort: the cocaine users, the lovers of opium and narcotics in general, addicts that succumbed to the ultimate state of decadence that a spirit, a creature of God, could fall into! They are in a lamentable state of vibrational depression. They are the true mental cases of the

spirit world. They are morally, mentally and spiritually wretched because their monstrous vices not only drained and killed their physical body, but extended the dreadful consequences of their abominable intemperance to their astral body, contaminating it with impurities and pestiferous influences that polluted it atrociously. "[68]

Camino saw these spirits and described them as "dazed, weepy, suffering, disheartened"[69]. He was told these misguided souls would be aided so they could at least understand their present situation and how they came to such a state. This is what Camino saw in the first part of the 1900's. Imagine the horde the spirit world receives every day in our present age, more than 100 years later. We now have giant pharmaceutical companies pushing mind altering drugs at us, new way to "get high" invented annually, and a culture that actively promotes such behavior as a desirable state.

## Reincarnation of Suicides

Camino wanted to know what will happen to them. He was told, they will reincarnate as they appear:

"Amid the suffering of the gloomy corners of the earth, and in the most wretched levels of society. Others will be the cancer-stricken, the paralytics, the mentally impaired, the hysterics, the convulsives, the incurable diseased beset with complexes that will challenge the noble science of earthly medicine... They will be an unpleasant burden on human society because they are the offspring of it and its wrongs; hence it is only fair that this same society house them and keep them as long as necessary – until such a calamitous situation is diminished!"[70]

Not only do we have to pay for our wrongs, but the society that encouraged the behavior must also recompense. The message is for those who attempt to flee life, whether by inducing themselves into a temporary forgetfulness of their circumstances or by ending their life. We are not allowed to skip school. We are put here on earth for a reason, and if we try to avoid that duty, we shall eventually be reminded of the consequences.

Camino was shaken by the prospect of a lifetime of punishment and asked, "If I understand correctly, is the punitive reincarnation that awaits these wretches simply forced on them by this section of our Department as a medical treatment? … Is it an antidote … a remedy?"[71] He received this answer:

> "Yes! It's just a medical treatment! A type of treatment that the urgency and gravity of the illness imposes on the patient! A dolorous procedure, but one we do not hesitate to use, because we know that only afterward will their real convalescence begin. However, it will not be a punishment per se, because no one will have inflicted punishment or handed down a sentence; on the contrary, all of us here who serve the Law will have made every effort allowable to bring relief to their dreadful situation. What it really is – really! – is *the effect of the cause that the patient himself created with the excesses he took pleasure in.*"[72]

Thankfully, Camino was told that Mary's hospital watched over each one and gave them constant care. When spirits were finished with their sojourn, the hospital took them back and prepares the spirits for a normal life, a life where they would be able to improve themselves.

## Reincarnation of Criminal Suicides

Next, Camino and his group walked through another ward full of more painful scenes, black terrible thoughts emanating from each of the patients. Camino wished to know why he senses such awful feelings from each of the bed ridden souls. His enquiry received an immediate response:

> "But how could it be otherwise? After all, they were the moral criminals; tormenters who, compelled by the turpitude of their own instincts, harmed and injured their neighbor; human monsters that satiated themselves with the misery they inflicted on the hearts and lives of others… How could rooms such as this one not be contaminated by darkness, when such darkness originated from inside these men; when they had taken pleasure in its folds, causing it and bringing it into their social

> and private lives, and then making it worse with the horrific blow of suicide?! … There they lay, in their sick beds, exactly as they had been while on earth: gallant men, seducers, deceivers, hypocrites, liars, corrupt, often occupying the highest positions in society."[73]

Reading this, when we hear of some high level criminal escaping their crime by suicide and think regretfully about how they adverted their just punishment, we now know differently. Their punishment is beyond what we could imagine. It is not just some time behind bars, where they will lose their freedom, but still get three square meals per day, but rather a lifetime to think about the possibilities of redemption. These criminals, whose last thought was that they were able to run away from all responsibilities, will be reincarnated as, "mentally-impaired, insane, epileptic, deaf and even blind individuals, … and in the degree equivalent to their crime."[74]

Even the weight of the crime will not preclude these spirits from receiving help in the physical world. The Hospital administrators report that many will be reincarnated close to mediums who will able to assist them to restore balance in their lives. Plus, they will be watched over by benefactors in the spirit world who lend assistance to all who attempt to find the right path.

Upon seeing the rows upon rows of the afflicted spirits, Camilo wondered why the punishment must be so harsh. After all people commit crimes every day. He was told, "Have you forgotten the tears these wretches made their brothers and sisters shed by inflicting them with torments caused by their selfishness and other vile expressions of their criminal hearts?"[75]

## "Pain", the Teacher

The path to redemption is long and laborious. We all must pay for what we sowed. In *The Spirits Book*;

> *999. Does sincere repentance during the earthly life suffice to efface the faults of that life, and to restore the wrong-doer to the favor of God?*

"Repentance helps forward the amelioration of the spirit, but all wrongdoing has to be expiated."[76]

Hence, there is no shortcut. No easy path for redemption. We can't lie our way out, we can't hire someone else to take the punishment, and there is no one to bribe to let us off the hook. We must pay the bill with our own time and labor.

At the end of the long tour through the wards of the truly pitiful spirits, Camino was told that all will recover eventually. The method of that recovery is described by those whose love and compassion will direct the care of the mournful spirits.

"Pain the Teacher will correct their anomalies and reconcile them with the Law! God is Infinite Mercy, my friends! He wants his people to live in harmony with the eternal beauty of his laws! And since we know that these laws are incorruptible, it is up to us to obey and respect them so that we don't wind up having to drink the bitter gall of the consequences that we created for ourselves with our freewill when we left the natural and luminous pathway."[77]

Does this seem harsh? That we have people with heart rendering disabilities around us, people who are wonderful friends suddenly die of an incurable disease, is a daily tragedy on this planet. The reason is that we are living on a planet of atonement, a place where we are learning to become better spirits, a place where, I am sure, all of us, have in some distant past, committed a heinous crime for which we too, had to pay a lifetime of debt.

Remember, most spirits, once they realize the extent of their wrongs, sign up and ask for their penance. Knowing that we all are immortal, it is natural for the wiser ones to discharge their debt by a seemingly brief (in the scheme of things), horrendous stay on earth. They do so with the aspiration to once more, after the trial, restart the ascent.

I will end with a message from the author, Yvonne Pereira, who in a footnote made this plea directly to all of us: "You, who are reading these pages! When you come across brothers or sisters suffering such abnormalities, do not shy away from silently praying in their presence: your harmonious vibrations will also be an excellent therapy!"[78]

# Chapter 10 – Interlude 2 – The Life of Amadeu Ferrari

In the book *Memoirs of a Suicide*, a group of recovering suicides are being brought forward in the lecture area to travel through their past lives to determine how they arrived at the life in which they committed suicide. Each person, one by one, is seated in a contraption at the front of the class. There is a type of screen, but it is more like a hologram, where the memories of the person in the chair become real to the entire audience.

The first person to experience the interrogation is Amadeu Ferrari. He had cancer, and to pay for his treatments he embezzled money from the bank where he worked. His cancer was attacking his tongue and throat. His previous life appears on the screen and is described as follows:

> "Amadeu appeared to us, depicted by his own mind, in the year 1840 as a trafficker of black slaves from Angola to Brazil... He was from Portugal, which explained our affinity for him. By means of a series of voyages, he enriched himself with the abominable trade, not sparing any efforts in his vile ambition of returning to Portugal as a millionaire. He inflicted indescribable torment on the wretches as he rounded them up in their free homeland to make slaves of them and handed them over to other ignoble accomplices sharing the same deranged ambitions! In the truculence of inhumane conduct, he excelled in the mistreatment of his captives, ordering them to be flogged for the most insignificant wrong, or even for no wrong at all.... Once, on one of his plantations, he raped a black slave who was little more than a child. Her poor father was an elderly slave sixty-years of age. In a moment of supreme suffering before the body of his child, who had chosen death to hide her shame, he had condemned Amadeu's vile act, accusing him of his daughter's suicide. In retaliation, Amadeu ordered cruel farm hands to burn the old slave's tongue with a red-hot iron until he collapsed in convulsions of agony."[79]

Fast forward, to Portugal, where Amadeu dies a rich man. He finds himself in the jungle surrounded by his old mistreated slaves. He spends years there tormented by all around him until one night, the old slave, Felicio, wjose he had burned, comes up to him and says, "Come, master, get up... let's leave this place."[80] Felicio had forgiven him and came to free him from those who had not learned how to let go of the desire for revenge.

The instructor explains to the audience that many of the slaves came from past lives as oppressors. Felicio, in his capacity working for the Roman Emperor Hadrian, committed many crimes and therefore paid his penance as a slave.

At the end of the interrogation, the instructor revealed a surprise for Amadeu:

> "At a signal from Epaminodas (the instructor), a side door had silently opened and Felicio appeared, serene and grave, and walked towards his former master... Now in possession of his entire past, Amadeu looked at him in terror... Slowly and imperceptibly, Felicio transformed himself using the power of his will - which easily changes the configuration of the astral body - and let himself be seen in his role as Romulo Ferrari, Amadeu's father!"[81]

The machinations of the spirit world are a wonder to behold. When you read about the relationships that have been set up in the spirit world for us incarnates, it makes you think, "Who exactly are my mother and father, brothers and sisters, and other relations?" We are all intertwined in the business of forgiveness, learning and salvation. We should look around and try to determine who we are having trouble with right now and what extra effort we should make to be at peace with those individuals.

# Chapter 11 - Reincarnation and Families

People wonder whether we have many families, mothers, fathers, and so on as we travel through multiple lives. How do we manage having a menagerie of relatives while in the spirit world? The answer is: We don't. Read on and find out why.

Most of us love our families, and our fondest wish is to be reunited with them in the spirit world. We may ponder what life would be like in a heavenly place with our loved ones. Then we think about reincarnation and realize that we may have had multiple families, including many different mothers and fathers and who knows how many brothers and sisters. So, is there a legion of relatives waiting for us, so that many we would need a terabyte size address book to keep them straight? Allan Kardec's book *The Gospel According to Spiritism* gives us the answer. In it we find this clarification:

> "Family ties are not destroyed by reincarnation, as certain persons believe; on the contrary, they are strengthened and become tighter."[82]

How can that be? How can we travel through countless centuries and somehow remain involved in our close family circle? The answer, like the answers to many other questions, lies in the Law of Affinity. Whereby, Souls who are at the same level share in a mutual affection, and have similar tastes naturally gather together.

## Law of Affinity - Like associates with Like

The Law of Affinity is actually one of the great filters, or more aptly, sorters, of the universe. Where souls more interested in doing harm gather in darken areas, souls who have respect and admirations for one another's achievements also grouped together in celestial cities. Allan Kardec explains how affiliated souls tend to stay with each other:

"These spirits happy at being together, seek out one another. Incarnation separates them only momentarily, because after their reentry into the errant state they meet again like friends who have returned from a journey. Frequently, they even follow one another into incarnation, wherein they are reunited in the same family or the same circle, working together for their mutual advancement."[83]

The tight cluster of souls will watch out for each other. While some are incarnates on earth, others will look on from high and help guide the spirits going through their trials. Each helps everyone in the group to advance together. As they become purer, their friendship becomes more concrete, as their bodies divest themselves of matter. Petty jealousies and selfishness don't disrupt their relationships.

There are different types of family relationships, including those in which one is bonded together with another due to a purely physical connection. Or a person we marry, not because of true spiritual affection, but of a sensual or monetary attraction. These are people who have been selected for us in order to experience the trials, that, need I remind you, we have selected ourselves. We may not like them very much, but I can guarantee we will learn some hard lessons from them and for that we should be grateful. As Allan Kardec states, "There are no lasting affections except spiritual ones; physical affections die out with the cause that gave rise to them; but that cause no longer exists in the world of spirits, whereas the soul exists forever".[84]

Therefore, when we feel a special kinship to select members of our family, most probably because we are united in the spiritual world, we should feel safe since they will always have our best interest at heart. On the other hand, those relations toward whom feel mistrustful are usually there for one of two reasons. First, they may be of an inferior level and require the love and guidance of advanced family members to assist them in improving their position. Who hasn't seen families where all of the children seem well brought up by good parents, except one, the black sheep? Now you have a likely explanation. The parents may have volunteered to help a poor soul improve his or herself only to find that in spite of their efforts, that spirit insisted in continuing with his or her old habits or tendencies.

A second reason for those difficult relatives is that they may be located with us as a trial. They may be poor souls that we have wronged in the past who are now introduced to us as a means of reconciliation to repair the damage we caused. Hopefully, a complete reconciliation will occur and whatever past recriminations that had existed will now be forgotten. Allan Kardec backs up this thought with this statement:

> "God, whose laws are all supremely wise, does nothing useless. Through reincarnation on the same globe, God has willed that the same spirits come in contact with one another again for the chance to repair their mutual offenses. Because of their previous relationships, God wishes furthermore to establish family ties on a spiritual basis and to support the principles of solidarity, fraternity and equality as a natural law."[85]

Hence, have no worries about our loved ones. While there may be more than you originally thought, you have the capacity to love many. You can also love with a purity of spirit, unencumbered by physical tethers, for your love is not based on any material calculation but on shared experiences and beliefs, a pure affection. Look forward to reuniting with your friends in the spirit world, to talking about what you learned and how you failed. Together, you can plan out your next physical adventure with the knowledge that you will have support both from heaven and from "on the ground".

# Chapter 12 – Why are There Difficult People in Your Life

Do you experience problems with some of your family members and have no idea why? Perhaps you have tried everything and they still just don't like you? Or worse, they are nice to you and you can't help but to reject them? There are explanations. As part of your learning experiences on earth, you have been reborn with past adversaries. For example they may have been rivals or people who assaulted you, or the explanation may be one of a myriad of other reasons for that indistinct feeling of revulsion.

We are all here on earth for a reason. According to Spiritism, codified by Allan Kardec, in his book *The Spirits Book*, we come to inhabit our physical bodies to improve ourselves, as part of our quest to become better souls, with the goal of someday becoming pure spirits and casting off our need for reincarnation. However, in the meantime, here we are. And, most amazingly, we're here with people we have known before in a previous life. *The Spirits Book* tells us:

> *204. As we have had many existences, do our relationships extend beyond our present existence?*
>
> "It cannot be otherwise. The succession of their corporeal existences establishes among spirits a variety of relationships which date back from their former existences; and these relationships are often the cause of sympathies or antipathies which you sometimes feel towards persons whom you seem to meet for the first time."[86]

Hence, like the episodes of a family drama on TV, the plot lines of our own stories continue from one life to the next. As an example, in a lecture given by Geraldo Lemos Neto, he tells of the cast of characters in the book, *Fifty Years Later*, inspired by the spirit Emmanuel, psychographed by Francisco C. Xavier, which describes a noble Roman, his life at the time, fifty years after Christ came, and the women who vied for his affections. One woman in particular, who loved him deeply and attempted to take him from his wife, is our main subject. Geraldo tells us that in a successive life, this woman was reborn as his sister. While she was a very good and loving person, she found every woman her brother attempted to have a relationship with, was lacking, and when he did marry, she never tired of pointing out that his wife was continually inadequate. The spirit world deliberately placed her in a sibling relationship with the man she had desired throughout hundreds of years, so she could learn the value of caring for others above herself, as well as self-discipline and restraint in her emotions.

## Love Triangle and Murder

Reincarnation can also play a part in our current life. In the book *And Life Goes On*, by the spirit Andre Luiz, psychographed by Francisco C. Xavier, a young man, Caio Serpa, murdered a rival, Tulio, to gain his first wife. While Caio's first wife, Evelina, was dying, Caio took up a relationship with Vera. Caio married Vera soon after Evelina's death. The spirit world worked to bring about the reunion of Caio and his victim Tulio.

As part of the plan for Tulio's next life they wanted him to be reborn as Caio's son, so the two could be reconciled. But they started the process very subtlety:

> "Tulio was taken to Vera one night when Serpa wasn't home so that he could get to know a bit about the woman who would receive him in her arms as a mother.
>
> As he watched her sewing in her Vila Mariana home, Tulio immediately felt drawn to her. He noticed her gentle face, the serene eyes of someone who had suffered much, and her skillful hands at work. Enchanted, he took in the peaceful atmosphere."[87]

Notice, they did not reveal who would be the father to Tulio. The spirit world works to free everyone from the petty hatreds and crimes of passions. Realizing this, the following Bible verse comes to mind and is now much clearer in its meaning:

"But I say to you who hear, Love your enemies, do good to those who hate you, bless those who curse you, pray for those who abuse you. To one who strikes you on the cheek, offer the other also, and from one who takes away your cloak do not withhold your tunic either. Give to everyone who begs from you, and from one who takes away your goods do not demand them back. And as you wish that others would do to you, do so to them." [Luke 6:27-36]

That Biblical text makes much more sense now, doesn't it, for in the awareness of reincarnation, we understand the long term plan. In our quest for moral perfection, we must shed our thirst for revenge, let go of our targeted hatred and be calm in the knowledge that when a person does a wrong, the all-powerful natural laws of God will enable that person to recover their moral debts and eventually better themselves. It is not up to us to be the judge. It is up to us to be reconciled with and compassionate toward those who didn't know any better when they committed their wrongs.

Getting back to the story from "Life Goes On", the spirit helper then implanted the idea of motherhood into Vera, who reacts positively to this suggestion:

"How I would love to have a son!" she thought, "How I long to be a mother!" She was awaiting this blessing from the Almighty; he surely wouldn't forget her! … Moreover, fully aware that her husband desired an heir for the future, in her daydream she intentionally prayed to God for a boy!"[88]

Taking care of both sides of the equation, the plan for Tulio's rebirth is complete. The beginning of a new life would heal the old wounds and the circle of karma will start to turn. The expected outcome of the placement of the victim into the perpetrator's house was explained as follows:

"Based on the truth of what they had been promised, Tulio would reincarnate with Caio Serpa as his father, totally magnetized by his mother's devotion, so that he could be around his former adversary once again and transform resentment into love by means of the therapy of forgetfulness."[89]

Will the father-son relationship be easy? Probably not, since deep down in his own instincts, Tulio will feel a tinge of resentment toward his father. This will have to be solved by the both of them, mainly by Caio, since he is the father and the guide for his son.

### A Crime for Money

Some relationships that are carried over from previous existences can be very complicated. However, the spirit world always delivers justice, as you shall see. In the book *In the Greater World*, by the spirit Andre Luiz, psychographed by Francisco C. Xavier, there is a man named Fabricio who betrayed his father's last wishes and stole the entire inheritance from his brothers, leaving them penniless. On his deathbed, we view the following scene, where Fabricio calls for his grandson, little Fabricio:

"My little Fabricio, I want you to pray for me when I die."

The boy didn't hesitate.

He knelt down right there and reverently said the Lord's Prayer.

When the prayer ended, the sick man asked with moist eyes:

"Dear child, don't forget to pray for me when I die."

The boy, now standing, hugged his grandfather and replied, weeping discreetly:

"You're not going to die!"

Appearing relieved, the old man responded to the affectionate gesture, gazed at his grandson and asked with a strange brilliance in his eyes:

"Little Fabricio, do you believe that God forgives sinners like me?"

The tearful and confused boy answered:

"Grandpa, I believe that God forgives all of us."

Displaying the anxieties that populated his soul, he asked further:

"Even a man who betrays his father's trust and steals from his brothers?"

The grandson hesitated, incapable of understanding the full extent of that intentional question. But wishing to please the patient any way he could, he uttered with complete childlike simplicity;

"I think God always forgives."

"That's what I wanted to know," stressed the elderly man, more relieved.[90]

Here is a man, a criminal, who lived out a long life in luxury, surrounded by a loving family. Who wouldn't think he had escaped all punishment and that his brothers and father were a few of many in a long line of unavenged victims.

He would not escape expiation and the wronged parties would get their repayments. For little Fabricio is actually the reincarnated spirit of his grandfather's father, as the book explains:

"The boy is Fabricio's former father. He has returned to the family of his criminal son through the blessed gates of reincarnation. He is his only grandson, and later he will assume control of the material inheritance of the family – the property that was his in the first place. The Law never sleeps."[91]

Not only would the money revert to its rightful owner, but the older Fabricio would have to go through his own trials even after death, as is explained:

"With the residues of his criminal actions in his mind, right after abandoning his physiological domicile, our sick friend will experience the results of his failure for a long time. This will continue up to the point where suffering will finally remove the malignant elements that poison his soul."[92]

As demonstrated, no one goes unpunished. Perhaps at some future date, the elder Fabricio may be reincarnated back into his family, or they may leave him behind, advancing spiritually while Fabricio remains mired in his materialistic desires.

## Try to Come to an Understanding

The combinations and permutations of concurrent and related lives of intersecting people, over eons, are endless. Exactly what kind of preceding relationships we shared with the current members of our extended families is unknown to us, but this much is certain, over the eons of time that we have been perfecting ourselves, we have built up a large reservoir of loved ones. This include people that we naturally gravitate toward, precisely according to the Law of Affinity, by which those of the same level of goodness and understanding are drawn together.

For the vast majority of us, these allies are more numerous than our adversaries. Therefore, seek out your estranged relations and attempt to come to an agreement or understanding with them, and let there be eternal peace between you, because it is for this reason that person was chosen to be in your circle. Failing to do so may require you to endure the same antipathy again in the next life.

Remember, you have friends here on earth, living beside you, as they have done lifetimes before. You also have friends who have moved on but are still watching over you and are interested in your advancement. As *The Spirits Book* says:

> *488. Have the relatives and friends who have gone before us into the other life more sympathy for us than spirits who are strangers to us?*
>
> "Undoubtedly they have; and they often protect you as spirits, according to their power."

*Are they sensible of the affection we preserve for them?*

"Very sensible; but they forget those who forget them."[93]

Let the help you are given percolate through your soul to give you strength during times of frustration with others. Know always that if you ask for the power to forgive, it will be granted.

# Chapter 13 – Interlude 3 - The Past Life of Joseph Mery

According to information on Wikipedia, Joseph Mery was a writer of stories, satires, and plays. He lived in France, was born in 1797 and died in 1866.He was an acquaintance of Alexandre Dumas, who wrote the *Count of Monte Cristo* and many other famous works.

As I read Spiritist books and encounter new names, I always look them up. You never know where the search will take you. Once, I read a passage in one of Andre Luiz books and saw the name of Emanuel Swedenborg referenced in a speech by a spirit who was lecturing about the difficulty of communicating from the spirit world to us on earth. I then went on to read some of Swedenborg books about his travels to the spirit realm.

Joseph Mery was mentioned in a book by Leon Denis, *Life and Destiny*. Leon was providing examples on past lives, and he talked about the past lives of Joseph Mery.

> "He had singular theories which to him were convictions. He firmly believed he had lived several times and recalled small incidents of anterior existences. He said Virgil and Horace had been friends of his, and he had known Augustus and Germanicus, and had fought in Gaul and Germany. He was a general, and commanded German troops. When they crossed the Rhine, he recognized places in the mountains where his name was Minius, and he gives an incident to substantiate his idea. One day Mery was visiting the Library of the Vatican in Rome; he was met by two young men in long brown robes, who spoke him in pure Latin. Mery was a Latin scholar, but he had never attempted to converse in the language of Juvenal. But as he listened to these young men, and admired their magnificent idiom, a veil seemed to fall from his eyes, and it seemed to him that it was thus he had conversed of old with his friends. Irreproachable phrases fell from his lips! Immediately he found elegant and correct expressions. He spoke in Latin as

he spoke in French. This he could not have done without apprenticeship. He must have journeyed through a century of splendor to have acquired such language, which could not have been attained in an hour."[94]

We never know where our instincts will take us. After all, we have learned that our conscience and our instincts are the product of the sum total of our previous lives. Imagine the hidden potential that lies within us and the possibilities we could step into if we could harness that wisdom.

This is why we occasionally hear about people who have had an accident or a medical procedure and suddenly they exhibit a new talent, such as speaking a different language or revealing an in depth knowledge about a subject they had never studied before (in this lifetime). The fact that we are reincarnated and are connected to the spirit world by our perispirits explains many of the anomalies that we see in the world.

# Chapter 14 – How the Process of Reincarnation Improves Us

What is the process to turn our raw souls into productive spirits? How are we molded, "scolded", and cajoled into conformance while retaining our personal identity? Well, God waits patiently for his natural laws to perform their magic. We are actually strapped in a ride that never stops and provides twists, turns, and enough g-force to transform us into an intelligent and useful member of the community of God's children.

If you don't believe in God, then examining the process to "hatch" new spirits, quasi civilize them, train them over eons, and patiently keep circulating them through the reincarnatory process until they become a pure spirit, ready to follow the doctrine of Spiritism with élan, should convince you that a higher intelligence is at work in the universe. How does the spirit realm turn out intelligent and productive spirits who are responsible for guiding planets like ours to a better sphere? By the way, the fact that I am neither intelligent nor industrious hasn't stopped me from writing is, for me, proof that I am here on earth for a reason.

## How Not to Create the Process of Improvement

Let's start with a thought experiment. Suppose you are the leader of a large corporation and wish to have the perfect work force. How would you go about creating the people to be able to perform all of the required functions, from janitor to accountant to manager? Keep in mind that you must perform every one of them with dedication to to your corporation. In fact, even more than being dedicated, you must have every fiber committed to your cause. For added effect, you are also omnipotent and can do anything you please. Here are some possibilities:

1. Find a perfect model, clone that and destroy the rest – This, in a nutshell, is how our modern day manufacturing works for goods produced. It functions pretty well, as long as close attention is

paid to quality. The downside is that, as we detect in nature, a colony of exact or near exact copies are prone to extinction. One catastrophic event, a rogue virus for example, would topple over the edifice, since all of the parts are equal and there are no reinforcing pillars to hold steady against a once in a millennia occurrence.

2. Rigorously train and indoctrinate your work force, but when a defective model is spotted, eliminate it. – This is a model of how many dictatorships and communist states attempt to control their citizens. Unfortunately, for those harried executives in charge, the constant use of resources to discover mal-functioning people is a heavy price to pay and has the effect of de-moralizing the rest, since the constant images of fellow workers disappearing seems to have a negative influence on the others.

3. Create a group of learning automatons who are genetically and intellectually diverse, wherefore each, depending on its environment attains varied levels of capabilities, while simultaneously weeding itself out and maintaining a positive attitude. But, and this is a big but, all would have to be absolutely dedicated and faithful to your corporation. What would be the rules to create such a force?

    a. All must grow their capabilities via training and attain the required certificates to demonstrate their readiness for the job.

    b. For those who are failing, or even actually attempting to divert the productivity of others, isolate and retrain them.

    c. Create a learning process whereby each absorbs all that is required while retaining individual characteristics that are not damaging to others in the group, and instead reinforce the group's positive behavior.

Wouldn't any modern corporation or government organization love to possess the capabilities listed above? Wouldn't be ideal to have a collection of employees, performing functions from the lowest level of difficulty to the highest, all with dedication, initiative, and absolute love for the highest authority.

## The Process

Well, while option three above is well beyond any organization based on earth today, the spirit world is using a variation of it and is filtering us through the process, turning out brilliant, competent, and loving souls. Creating a meritocracy beyond Plato's vision of his Republic. In Plato's Republic, the basis of training potential leaders, called guardians, is:

> "Guardians should be educated on these four virtues: wisdom, courage, justice and temperance. They also suggested that the second part of the guardians education should be on gymnastics. With the physical training they will be able to live without getting medical attention often. In other words, the physical education or training will help prevent illness and weakness. In summary, Socrates asserts that both male and female guardians be given the same education, that all wives and children be shared and that ownership of private property ought to be prohibited amongst them. The following outlines stages that guardians should grow through before they are able to lead their people: Until 18, basic intellectual study and physical training. Followed by 2 years of military training. Followed by ten years of mathematics. At 30, five years of dialectic. Followed by 15 years as leaders, trying to 'lead people from the cave' (note, this is figurative, not literal). Upon reaching 50, they are fully aware of the form of the good and totally mature - ready to lead!"[95]

Socrates, who was a herald to the doctrines of Jesus, was influenced by his remembrances and communication with the Spirit world. He intuitively knew the eons spent in successive lives, learning, suffering and preparation to purify each spirit.

God has set this process by his natural laws. Laws such as for every action there is a reaction, do unto others as you would have them do unto you, and others. But the constant organizer, the filter, the driver which is at the controls is the Law of Affinity. Like attracts like, a simple concept, but one which is indescribably powerful. For all who reach the various spiritual levels are tied to the Law. The Law of Affinity groups the dedicated and loving together, as well as the corrupt and rebellious. For the very thoughts and actions a spirit commits places that spirit in the correct category. When a good spirit commits a wrong act, or generally doesn't fit in, that spirit will automatically descend to a retraining area, where they will determine, on their own, the course to take to re-ascend.

What could be more beautiful than the machine, controlled by the coded Laws, hurtling us into an ever contracting filter as we ascend, periodically re-working our imperfections, where each individual spirit eventually comes out, as separate characters, all with distinct personalities, but at a comparable level of overall goodness and capacity to love.

## Our Training

Each spirit must begin somewhere, and where better than to send them to a place in which they are exposed to the worse conditions imaginable, a primitive planet. Imagine, as a young child, landing in the midst of a tribe of headhunters. You would learn the most basic of survival skills, while also schooled in the rudimentary social abilities to function as a team member. Pain would instruct you about the results of putting your hand in fire, killing others without a good back-up plan to escape and other valuable lessons. Training to love your neighbor is minimal at this junction.

At some point in time, in the early adolescent of your spirit hood, you graduate to a semi-organized civilization. Written laws and informal codes of conduct assist you in controlling your basic instincts. The beauty of this period is the patience in which we are conducted through this phase. As we move forward and sometimes backwards, we may spend time in the lower regions, where other bad spirits subject us to what we did to others on earth. Thereby, indelibly absorbing the basic lesson of the golden rule. Upon exiting the lower realms, the lesson is reinforced by a life marked by suffering at critical milestones, again the tool that always works to focus our thoughts, pain, transforms our attitude, and so upon leaving the body, our perispirit, has realized new and valuable lessons. Thusly, setting us up nicely for our next leap forward.

Once, we have conformed to the basic decencies of life and are committed, while in the spirit world, to follow the Spiritist Doctrine, once again, we are thrust into life, to gain multiple levels of valuable experience. We may be rich in one life, poor in another, famous for just cause, or famous for being a passing fad, all valuable lessons. For in order to be whole, to remain calm in all environments, we must have our instincts prepared for every type of situation. Our instincts are with us during each life, guiding us, along with our conscience, along our intended path to purity.

Hence, the reason for the many vicissitudes in our life, the bumpier the road, the more we learn that the up and downs equal themselves out, and in the end we are left with our sense of honor and the comforting feeling of the good that we have accomplished.

All with the expressed purpose to filter out our propensity for materialism, selfishness and pride. When we begin to demonstrate the first signs of real progress, we are given missions to accomplish positive influences on earth. A test, the vast majority of us fail, but as with our initial trials, we pick ourselves up, fortify our minds with greater determination and try again. Our gentle instructors attempt to give us tasks that we are able to accomplish, but like the children that we are, our capacity to make wrong choices is breathtaking. Eventually, as rookies everywhere learn, you become a veteran, learn the system and begin to be worth the effort spent for your previous training.

As we rise, our capabilities increase, the Law of Affinity, places us amongst our precise set of peers, so our correct behavior will be reinforced at every turn. At each step, more blemishes are removed. There may be an infinite number of imperfections to burn-out; don't worry the process is perfect, all will be discovered, and plans to repair each deficiency have been drawn-up and made ready for further implementation.

### We Will Arrive Eventually

The process that we must survive, for we will, since we are immortal, is similar to turning pig iron into steel. We don't have the luxury of going into the furnace only once, but thousands of times, like the forging of ancient Samurai swords, ten thousand strikes of the hammer on the sword against the anvil and countless burnings into the near-heat of the sun. For only pain truly transforms our soul. Only pain makes us realize our fundamental errors and provides the motivation to unalterably change. Our training, our reincarnations, is a form of legalized torture to mold us into pure and powerful spirits. This may sound cruel, but given the authority and supremacy of an advanced spirit, would you have it any other way? What could an unrepentant, hateful and envious pure spirit do to the universe? The damage would be incalculable.

For a pure spirit, the mere spark of a thought causes action. Hence, these invincible tools, for good, can't be permitted to have a single flaw. Like a diamond, whose formation may take millions of years, under the crushing weight of the earth, a spirit must emerge absolutely perfect.

For this is the reason, why we, as poor vessels of imperfection, are so loved by those higher. They understand, with the true empathy of walking in our shoes, the difficulties that lay ahead us, and what we went through. Therefore, while we may entertain our brief periods of rebelliousness, in the end we intuitively comprehend the requirement to learn and immolate ourselves into the fire, to rise once more just a little bit better than before.

# Chapter 15 – Introduction to Spiritism

I want to give you good news and then bad news. First, the good news, you are immortal. Your spirit will live forever. You will experience life after life in a quest to perfect yourself. You have a mission, the most important mission possible; to improve, to love, to be charitable. To be part of a grand plan to not only raise yourself, but your neighbors and the entire human race.

Now the bad news; for every wrong you commit, your will have to pay for it in this life or the next. And, the trials you are experiencing now are the results of errors you have committed in the past, plus a splattering of coursework that you have been assigned.

How do we know all of this?

### Jesus promised us more Information

> "If you love me, keep my commands. And I will ask the Father, and he will give you another Consoler to help you and be with you forever…the Spirit of Truth. The world cannot accept him, because it neither sees him nor knows him. But you know him, for he lives with you and will be in you." New Testament John 14: 15-17

> "But the Consoler, the Holy Spirit, whom the Father will send in my name, will teach you all things and will remind you of everything I have said to you." New Testament John 14: 26

You saw these Bible verses at the beginning of the book, but since they are the herald announcing the advent of Spiritism, they bear repeating. For the Spirit of Truth, after eighteen hundred years finally arrived, to let us know to start our preparation for the next stage of humanity.

What did the Consoler actually do? What did he contribute? Spiritism states that Allan Kardec was the Codifier, who presented the Spirit of Truth (Consoler) and that in the five books that Allan Kardec assembled, he revealed the extent of the Spirit world, who is God and Jesus, why we are here on earth, how we should live and the doctrine to follow. That is all. The answers to questions that every one of us have spent nights pondering.

## Allan Kardec

To start at the beginning, because that is the logical place, Allan Kardec is the pen name of the French teacher and educator Hippolyte Léon Denizard Rivail (Lyon, October 3, 1804 – Paris, March 31, 1869).[96] Wikipedia describes his early life:

> Rivail was born in Lyon in 1804. He was raised as a Catholic. He was a disciple and collaborator of Johann Heinrich Pestalozzi, and a teacher of mathematics, physics, chemistry, astronomy, physiology, comparative anatomy and French in Paris. For one of his research papers, he was inducted in 1831 into the Royal Academy of Arras. He organized and taught free courses for the underprivileged.[97]

Allan Kardec was fifty-one years old when he first encountered spirits. Anna Blackwell, who translated his books into English in 1881, describes his first encounters and what set him off in his journey:

> When, about 1850, the phenomenon of "table-turning" was exciting the attention of Europe and ushering in the other phenomena since known as "spiritist", he quickly divined the real nature of those phenomena, as evidence of the existence of an order of relationships hitherto suspected rather than known, namely, those which unite the visible and invisible worlds. Foreseeing the vast importance, to science and to religion, of such an extension of the field of human observation, he entered at once upon a careful investigation of the new phenomena. A friend of his had two daughters who had become what are now called "mediums." They were gay, lively, amiable girls, fond of society, dancing, and amusement, and habitually received, when "sitting" by themselves or with their young companions, "communications" in harmony with their worldly and somewhat frivolous disposition. But, to the surprise of all concerned, it was found that, whenever he was present, the

messages transmitted through these young ladies were of a very grave and serious character; and on his inquiring of the invisible intelligences as to the cause of this change, he was told that "spirits of a much higher order than those who habitually communicated through the two young mediums came expressly for him, and would continue to do so, in order to enable him to fulfill an important religious mission."[98]

He was extremely interested in this message of a mission and wished to delve deeper. He discussed how he could ask and organize a series of questions to get a more complete understanding of the spirit world with his wife. His wife, Amelie, encouraged him to undertake this task. Given his background, he organized a series of questions that would be posed by mediums to spirits. Allan Kardec was not a medium himself, so he used the service of various mediums to gather the information. He did not rely on one reply, but made sure that an answer to one question was seconded by another medium in a different location.

Allan Kardec wrote five books (The Spirits' Book, 1857; The Mediums' Book, 1861; The Gospel according to Spiritism, 1864; Heaven and Hell, 1865; Genesis, 1868), each dealing with separate subjects, but at the same time overlapping in their complete description of the Spiritist doctrine. The first and most famous is the book that he was given the title by his spirit messengers.

## What is Spiritism?

The basic tenants of Spiritism are:

1. Love God.
2. Do unto others as you would have others do unto you.
3. Practice justice.
4. Forgive all who offend you.
5. Make amends for our own wrong doing.

The spirits revealed to us the basic facts of our existence:

1. Your soul is immortal.
2. You travel through multiple lives as a process to learn to love, be fraternal, and be selfless.
3. The goal of God is for every spirit is to one day be pure.
4. There is no eternal hell, it is a station for souls who are materialistic and have an excessive love of self.
5. There are many levels of heaven. Heaven is not a place where we have eternal leisure, but one of on-going work to help others.
6. Life on earth is like a school. You are assigned events in your life and how you react and behave will determine your spiritual progress.

In the 1930's in Brazil, the medium Chico Xavier began psychographing (the process of a medium writing under the direction of a spirit) messages and books sent by spirits. From the very beginning he was told to always follow the doctrines of Allan Kardec. Chico wrote more than 400 books by the time of his death in 2002. Within these books, the spirits revealed information about Allan Kardec and the spirit world's plan for our future;

1. When Jesus referred to the "Great Consoler", he was foretelling the arrival of the Spirit of Truth, which was codified by Allan Kardec.
2. For the earth to progress, the human race needs to understand that every action they do here on earth will have consequences in their next life.
3. The Bible was written by men under the influence of their beliefs and culture at their time. While the central spiritual message of love is eternal, the stories of the Bible, such as the Earth being made in

six days are allegories and not meant to be taken literally.

4. We are being told this now because the human race is culturally and technically advanced enough to be able to accept these messages.

5. Spiritism is not meant to replace religions, but to supplement them with the knowledge of the basic doctrine of reincarnation and its purpose.

6. The spreading and acceptance of Spiritism will enable to world to begin a new age, where war is a thing of the past.

7. The Spirit world has planned these events and is guiding the earth through subtle interventions.

8. At some time in the future, science will definitely prove the existence of a soul and an afterlife.

As one can see, the tenets of reincarnation have also been delivered to us via an alternative channel. That of the spirit world communicating directly to mediums to alert us of a life beyond our single human existence. While all around us people who have psychic abilities or those who had NDEs experiences are reporting the same philosophy of love and redemption through trials.

## What is Our Plan?

Discovering Spiritism leads one to the feeling that you are on a roller coaster and are unable to get off. The more you read, the more questions you have, then you try to find where they could be answered, but at the end you have a larger set of questions than when you started. The numerous questions could be separated into major categories. One of the most significant set of inquiries concerns the matter of your personal destiny. The discussion of the plan for your life on earth is scattered throughout Kardec's books and in psychographed books by mediums, such as Francisco C. Xavier.

In Allan Kardec's *The Gospel According to Spiritism*, the starting point for understanding your trials is in this paragraph, "Christ said, 'Blessed are the afflicted, for they shall be comforted'. But how can we bless suffering if we don't know why we suffer? Spiritism shows that the cause lies in previous existences and in the destiny of earth, where humans expiate their past. It shows them the purpose of their suffering as being salutary which lead to healing and which are the purification that ensures happincss in future existences. Humans understand that they deserve to suffer and they find suffering to be just. They know that this suffering aids their progress and they accept it without complaining, just as workers accept the work that will ensure their wages."[99]

Why is it important to understand our place in our destiny? According to the quote above, we should gladly accept whatever is thrown at us with a smile and work our butts off to get through it. Well, except for the few of us that possess that perfect attitude of accepting all of life's vicissitudes, we need to first comprehend what is occurring so we can meditate on it and try to mold our attitude so we may survive the ordeal the best that we can.

First the good news. We do have freewill. Although, I believe it is less than what is advertised. Why, because the Spirit world wants all of us charging ahead in life as well as we are able. And after all, you want to keep the troops motivated, don't you? The bad news, as stated in the beginning, is that you will be paying for your transgressions in past lives; there is no escaping that fact. So here is the hard part, how do you combine the expiation of your sins with making free-will choices and doing what you desire in your life? This is what the majority of the rest of the book is about.

# Chapter 16 – The Power of Thought

According to Spiritism, thought has power, it has consequences. How is this possible? In the book, *In the Domain of Mediumship (Life in the Spirit World)*, inspired by Andre Luiz, psychographed by Francisco C. Xavier, there are some explanations.

As we attempt to modify our behavior to improve our status, we must first learn to change our habits at the base; which is our thoughts, for we think first before any action and if we are able to create new habits, our battle is halfway won. Therefore, we must understand that indeed, our thoughts do have power.

Ever since we were children, we have been fascinated by the power of thought. Who, as a child, hadn't been worried that their thought caused, or could have triggered a bad action, whether it was in moments of anger against your parents, your dog, or another object of scorn? As we grew up, we learned to dismiss this idea, only primitive peoples still believed in the "evil eye" and other forms of spells. Although, for many of us, we still retained a belief in the power of positive thinking. This belief was more rooted in fashioning ourselves to achieve as opposed to guiding external events according to our desires. We also hoped for some of the latter, but never counted on it.

Accepting Spiritism radically changes this paradigm. We are told we do radiate our mental energies. In fact, we should be careful in what we think, because our thoughts do indeed have consequences.

How do we know all of this?

## Thoughts are Mental Telegrams

Be careful of our thoughts. They leave our minds and can draw in unwanted guests. Andre Luiz gives an example of this, in his book, *Workers of the Life Eternal*, where during a funeral; a group of people were talking about the deceased. One man started to reveal that the deceased knew of a man who committed murder, but never revealed the name, due to the high position of the murderer. Andre Luiz describes what happened next:

> "At that moment, a horrendous figure followed by others no less monstrous, appeared unexpectedly. The figure approached the thoughtless commentator, and upon hearing his last words, shook him, crying out;
>
> 'I'm the murderer! What do you want from me? Why have you called me? Are you a judge?'
>
> The narrator was unable to see what I could, but his body was shaken by an involuntary shudder, which drew muffled laughter from all those present."[100]

Examples, such as this one, are a constant theme in literature inspired by Andre Luiz. Our thoughts are radio waves, indiscriminately radiated in all directions. You never know what person or spirit will tune at what time. Additionally, do we completely understand the effect of our thoughts? When we think badly of someone, are we increasing that person's chance of failure? Training our minds to regulate our often chaotic thought ramblings must be one of the primary reasons we are obligated to live through numerous reincarnations.

## How does Our Thoughts Transmit?

In the book, *In the Domain of Mediumship*, Andre Luiz is investigating different types of mediumship. In one case, where a medium's (Raul) ability is amplified by the presence of a spirit, Clementino, Andre could detect the great increase in power in the medium's body. Andre's mentor catches his thoughts and supplies the answer:

> "Brother Clementino's mental forces acted upon the psyche of Raul, as electricity acts upon an electric bulb. Pressing upon the solar plexus, it rises toward the neuro-cerebral system, much like electricity from a power plant reaches a bulb, expanding through the incandescent filaments to produce

light."[101]

Hence, while our minds are a mini generator, our capacity can be amplified, by external forces, or by a combination of minds focusing together, as in prayer. This phenomenon has been detected by a group started at Princeton University. A team of researchers have place random number generators around the world. With the assumption that the number would always be random. They wanted to detect if events which caught the attention of the world, or in just some local places where the random number generators were located, could be modified by our collective mental energies. The effort is called The Global Consciousness Project.[102]

The method to detect the power of our mental energies is to compare the expected results of a wide spectrum of random number generators, which should have a relatively smooth pattern of random numbers spread across the world, to the actual results during an event. There are many such events described in their web pages. The most startling is the September 11th terrorist attack on the World Trade Center. Here is their commentary and graph:

> "The graph of data from the formal prediction for September 11 shows a fluctuating deviation throughout the moments of the five major events, during which ever-increasing numbers of people around the world are hearing the news and watching in stunned disbelief. Times of the major events are marked by boxes on the line of zero deviation. The uncertain fluctuation of the EGG data continues for almost half an hour after the fall of the second WTC tower. Then, at about 11:00, the cumulative deviation takes on a strong trend that continues through the aftermath period and ultimately exceeds the significance criterion. There were 37 eggs reporting on September 11, and over the 4 hours and 10 minutes of the prediction period, their accumulated Chisquare was 15332 on 15000 degrees of freedom. The final probability for the formal hypothesis test was 0.028, which is equivalent to an odds ratio of 35 to one against chance."[103]

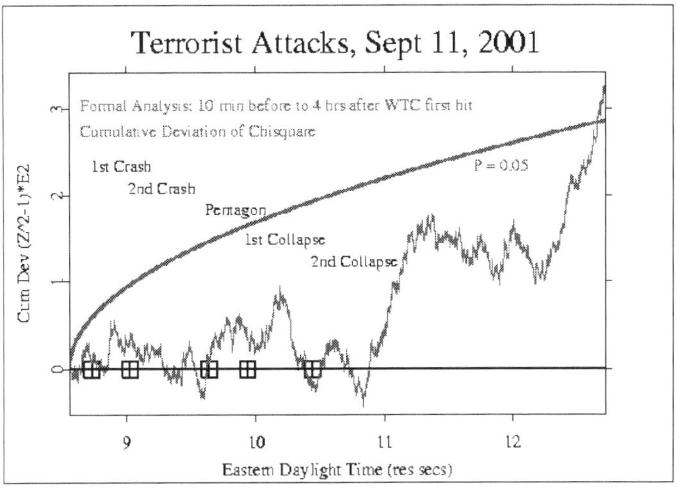


As one can see, as the event unfolded, the effect of our collective mental energies grew. Does this provide absolute proof? No, but it is an interesting assessment by a group that has no connection to Spiritism. A study that provides a hint that academia is interested in measuring our mental energy. These types of research are just beginning, who knows what else will be discovered in the future.

Back to Andre Luiz, he is interested in the analogy of our thoughts and the light bulb. He wishes to know how the energy of the light bulb is related to our mental forces. His instructor quickly perceived his thoughts and explained the relationship:

> "The bulb, in whose interior the light is produced, disperses the photons which are elements of nature that vibrate in physical movements particular to them. Our soul, in whose intimate ambient the radiating idea is processed, projects the condensed spiritual elements into various mental forces. The world acts one upon the other through the radiation they emit, and the souls influence one another via the mental agents they produce."[104]

Hence, our mind does send out energy, not photons, but another form, of which our science has not yet explained. The normal functioning of our body supplies the power, derived from our food intake, to allow our brains the electrical and chemical power for our neurons to trigger to internally form and emanate our thoughts. Andre takes this logic and extrapolates to its logical conclusion.

> "Just as we on Earth have an understanding of the chemistry of dense matter by cataloguing its atomic units, we can also study the make-up of the mind. Cruel thoughts, rebellion, sadness, love, comprehension, hope and happiness have individual weights and make the soul more dense or subtle, In addition, we can define it magnetic qualities. Each mental wavelength possesses its specific coefficients of energy expressed in silent concentration, speech or written word."[105]

If this statement is true, that by analyzing the wavelengths radiating from our minds, we are able to ascertain the general thoughts of a person, this explains how spirits are able to mentally read our minds. More worryingly, at some time in the future, a machine to read minds would be possible.

Hence, our thoughts result in real manifestations of power. They affect us and others around us, even into the spirit world, from the highest to the lowest regions. Andre Luiz sums up the importance of our minds.

> "We are victims or beneficiaries of our own thoughts according to the mental energies that we project. Thus, we enslave ourselves by our own erroneous thoughts or liberate ourselves toward progress, according to our decisions and activities, in harmony or disharmony with the eternal laws."[106]

And, remember, that as we modify our thoughts, we modify our perispirit, either elevating or falling in the quality of our contemplations, which following the Law of Affinity, whereby like attracts like, we are determining the level in which we will exist in the spirit realm. Reason enough to begin the long road to exercise our mental discipline.

# Chapter 17 - The Difference between Anger and Indignation

In the Spirit realm, it is taught to control emotions, for emotions cause actions. When we succumb to anger, the effects are not beneficial to anyone. But there are methods to use your thoughts and mental force to cause actions for the benefit of all.

In the books, authored by Andre Luiz and psychographed by Francisco C. Xavier, there are always nuggets of spiritual and practical information dispersed about. In the book *Between Heaven and Earth*, Andre Luiz is listening to an intimate classroom discussion given by Clara on the subject of the voice. She tells her students about the importance of the voice:

> "According to what we are learning this evening, speech, whatever it may be, invariably entails specific electrical energies, liberating rays of a dynamic nature. As we all know, the mind is the incessant generator of power through the positive and negative wires of the sentiment and the thought, thereby producing speech, which is an electromagnetic discharge regulated by the voice. That is why, in all of our areas of activity, the voice modulates speech. This requires the purification of the inner life, because speech, after the mental impulse, lies at the base of creation; thanks to speech, people approach and adjust themselves to the work they are responsible for, and by means of the voice, such work may be aided or retarded in space and time."[107]

The idea of the power of thought and our need to regulate that influence is a recurring theme. In the spirit world, and to an extent in the material world, we are our thoughts, but more importantly, our feelings affect the world around us. Our thoughts cause actions through the electrical vibrations generated by our mind. That power must be tightly measured. The need for controlling our emotions is backed by a question from a student, "When we want to deal with a problem, is it crucial that we never become angry?"[108]

## Anger

Clara provides the answer, “Yes it is. It’s a proven fact that anger never does anyone any good. Anger is nothing more than a dangerous short-circuit in our mental energies due to a defect in our emotive world, resulting in destructive rays being emitted all around us.”[109] Words to live by. How many of us fall into the trap of anger? I know I have lost control too many times to count. The quest for improving our inner emotional balance to create the required spiritual calmness to regulate our emotions is vital for us all.

And what exactly is the danger in being angry? Clara provides the details, “On such occasions, if we aren’t with someone who possesses the insulating material of prayer or patience, the sudden imbalance in our energies causes great harm, because, when thoughts of anger become interiorized, they can cause temporary mental blindness, dragging the mind into sensations rooted in the remote past, sensations that in turn drag us down into unfortunate experiences of lower animality without even realizing it. According to what we know, anger cannot and must not be expressed in what we say. An angry person is an out of control dynamo, and coming into contact with him or her may cause the strangest disturbances.”[110] Hence, not only do we emanate corrupt vibrations, but we inadvertently reinforce emotions from a more primitive past that we should have strived to remove from our repertoire.

## Indignation

As we all understand, there must be times when we need to express ourselves in a stern manner. How else, in certain situations, can we communicate the importance or urgency, of a point we are attempting to deliver. The dilemma is solved by a student’s question, “What if we were to replace the term ‘anger’ with ‘indignation’?”[111] As usual, Clara provides the answer:

> “Good point. We cannot finish our lesson without analyzing indignation as a state of the soul that is sometimes necessary. Of course, we must avoid excesses. Getting upset all the time

about petty things demeans the gifts of life, wasting them inconsequentially without the least advantage for oneself or for others. Let's imagine indignation as the raising of the tension in the power-plant of our organic resources, create special effects that enable us to carry out our tasks efficiently. In exceptional cases, when such a power difference impacts our daily life, we mustn't forget to control the inflection of our voice. Just as managing electrical energy requires monitoring the voltage, we need to monitor our indignation, especially when we have to express it by means of speech, projecting our voice only with enough power that can be used by those to whom we direct the charge of our sentiments. It is crucial for us to modulate the expression of what we are saying, just like the emission of electricity is modulated."[112]

With indignation we are using the power of our thought to amplify our force to accomplish two goals. The first is to enable us to focus our will power on the task at hand. The second is to direct the force of our thoughts and speech to the person we are trying to spur into action.

Clara concludes her lesson with a message on the need to always control ourselves:

"Our life may be compared to a lengthy learning course in whose innumerable classes we receive and give, help and are helped. In every circumstance, serenity is always the best adviser, but in a few aspects of our struggle, indignation is needed for us to express our being repulsed by deliberate acts of rebellion against the Laws of the Lord. During this elevated mental tension, however, we must never give way to violence and we must never lose our dignity, as we've received from the Divine Trust the gift of higher knowledge. Thus, it is enough for us to abstain from acts that we inwardly disapprove of, because our attitude is a magnetic induction current. All around us, whoever is attuned to us usually does what he or she sees us do. Consequently, what we do is a center of attraction. Thus, we need to be very careful about what we say during moments of high tension in our emotional world so that our voice does not come out in wild cries or cruel remarks that are no more than hurtful shocks to others, sowing thorns of antipathy and revolt that are harmful to what we are supposed to be doing."[113]

Therefore, we are all radio towers, emitting thoughts and emotions to all around us. What we send out over the airwaves can be used for good or cause chaos. We all have a level of personal responsibility, not only to ourselves, but to the world at large around us, to expand our ability to control our emotions and channel them for positive purposes.

# Chapter 18 – Interlude 4 – The Past Life of Alfred and Ismalia

The story of Alfred and Ismalia isn't actually about their past lives. It's about their life in the spirit world after their incarnated lives. The story illustrates that true love survives many trials and separations and that if a couple are bonded together, no one deed, neither life nor death keeps them apart for long.

In the book, *The Messengers*, inspired by the spirit Andre Luiz and psychographed by Francisco C. Xavier, there is a spirit, Alfred, who tells how, when he was incarnated, was a successful businessman. He threw himself into his business dealings and was quite wealthy. His negotiations and the running of his business was complex, which kept him away from his wife, Ismalia and his children. He goes on to tell the crux of the story:

> "Ismalia was the stronghold of my neglected family. Virtue, however, can always be tormented by vice, and I let my wife be sexually harassed by a disloyal friend, someone with whom I shared extensive business interests. Ismalia suffered in silence for years until he finally realized that he was getting nowhere with his immoral propositions."[114]

Alfred's business partner then started to persuade him that women in general weren't trustworthy. Slowly Alfred's deceitful friend began zeroing in on Ismalia. The constant drone of the possibilities of Ismalia unfaithfulness started to wear Alfred down.

Alfred would watch the smallest detail in everything Ismalia did, analyzing her behavior and actions for clues. He imagined the slightest deed she performed to be proof of her guilt.

Ismalia, knowing Alfred's friendship for his business partner, never revealed the story of the unwanted sexual advances to Alfred. She suffered in silence.

As usual in these cases, where there is a breakdown in communication, Alfred became a tyrant around the house and he would accuse her of being unfaithful. She only responded in silence.

### The Plot by Ismalia's Harasser

Alfred then tells of his partner's next deed:

> "Finally, still not pleased with his results, my business associate hired a stranger to invade our home and remain in hiding in the room next door to our bedroom. I noticed something out of the ordinary, and burst into the bedroom like a madman. Ismalia, who had been lying in bed, begged me to calm down while I tore the room apart, looking for her supposed lover. Suddenly I saw the shadow of the stranger, who fled from the room next door, out the window, and into the garden, without my having been able to get a hold of him. I ran behind him with a gun, shooting in different directions, but did not hit him."[115]

Alfred, fully releasing his pent up anger from many months, thought of killing Ismalia, but something stopped him from pulling the trigger. He did the next cruelest action, he arranged to take complete custody of the children and send Ismalia back to her parent's farm. She was not allowed to see the children again.

Alfred went alone to Europe to recover from his discovery. He arranged for the children to be taken care of by a governess. He made no attempt to find out the truth or get in touch with Ismalia. After two years in Europe, Alfred was in France, when he received a letter that after her complete abandonment, she fell ill and died of tuberculosis.

How tragic are our actions when we do not possess the capacity to love unconditionally. Spiritism teaches us that all have at one time or another played the victim and the betrayer. None of us are undeserving of sympathy.

### Example of True Understanding

An example of what our feelings should be is in the book, *In the Domain of Mediumship*, inspired by Andre Luiz and psychographed by Francisco C. Xavier, also known as Chico, there is a scene where a woman, Anesia, has asked for help from the Spiritual world. She is worried that her husband, Jovino, has found another woman. During her sleep, when she is out of her body, a team of spirits, led by Aulus, accompanies Anesia to where Jovino has met his girlfriend. Anesia sees the entire scene of Jovino drinking and showing displays of affection with the other woman.

Anesia is furious, cries and leaves the bar where she has witnessed her husband in the company of a rival. The Spiritual Team Leader, Aulus, follows her and says:

> "Dear sister, please take hold of yourself. You prayed so that you could receive spiritual assistance and we have answered your call. Cheer up! Don't lose hope."
>
> "Hope?" replied the poor woman, whose face was bathed in tears. "I am the object of treason."
>
> The conversation between them continued in a moving expressive tone.
>
> "Treason by whom?" asked Aulus.
>
> "By my husband, who failed in his marriage promises."
>
> Aulus tells her, "Do you believe that marriage is a simple excursion on Earth? Dear friend, the home is a school where souls reunite to achieve individual regeneration knowing that perfection is ours in the future. In educational establishments there are professors and students. Don't you know that the best ones should help those marching behind?"
>
> Upon hearing Aulus' words Anesia interrupted her laments. Yet, after looking at our mentor with intense confidence, she begins sadly; "But Jovino..."
>
> Aulus interrupted her, adding: "Are you forgetting that now is when your husband requires your understanding and affection? A woman should not always view her companion as the man

she loves tenderly, but as a spiritual son, who needs to be guided with understanding and sacrifice. Equally, a husband should not always contemplate his wife as the flower of his dreams, but rather as a daughter of his heart, who ask for tolerance and kindness, so that she can be taken from darkness to light."

"Anesia, love is not just rosy happiness and the sweet response to sex. It is a light that shines in the heights, inspiring the renunciation and unconditional pardon of those we love. Jovino is like a plant that God conveyed into your hands, and you must be a gardener. The plant will be attacked by parasites or deadly worms; however, there is no reason to fear if the gardener is attentive and vigilant."[116]

The books by Andre Luiz, constantly deliver the unexpected lesson, the Spiritist Doctrine applied to the ultimate level. Not just unconditional love, but a constructive love. A love where each of us has the responsibility to guide, not just strangers, but our closest relations, people who have the capacity to hurt us deeply.

## Alfred's Discovery

Alfred spent many years concentrating on his business and his children. He tried to repress the pass and forget all that had happened. Until one day:

"Years went by – until one day I was summoned to the home of my old business associate who was on his deathbed. Then and there he confessed what he had done, how he had harassed Ismalia and tricked me. He begged for my forgiveness, but I couldn't give it. I was devastated."

"That confession hit me hard. From that day on my life was that of a madman. I tried somehow to amend the effects of my wrongdoing by explaining the facts to Ismalia's parent. And after some time, I also returned to the spiritual world, laden with guilt, in very poor spiritual condition."[117]

After his death, Alfred spent some time wandering about

aimlessly in the lower zone. The place between the celestial cities where spirits ascend who are free of their material passions and understand the love of God and the depths where those who have criminal tendencies gather, for only as long as each one of them desires. Hence, many are in the lower zones, those who are not cruel, but so preoccupied by their left over earthly worries or never considered the possibility of an afterlife, they are unable to look up and see the plan for perfection before their eyes.

Alfred was finally rescued from his sojourn in the world in the middle of Heaven and Hell:

> "Needless to say and amazingly, I soon saw myself protected by Ismalia. Unfortunately for me, there is a wide void between Ismalia and myself. She follows my steps closely, but is a dweller of higher planes, which I still work hard to enter into. So, for a long time, I have been dedicating my efforts to assisting the unenlightened and the sufferers who come to this outpost. Ismalia comes once a month to help me out and encourage my efforts."[118]

The outpost that Alfred mentions is located in the lower zones, where good Samaritans find lost souls, those that don't realize they have passed away. The poor spirits who are still attached to their life on earth and don't realize the need to move on. For theses souls should be concentrating on their own spiritual progress instead of worrying about their possessions or left-behind family members. Only by raising themselves up first are they able to provide assistance to others.

Andre asks Alfred why couldn't Ismalia come down and help Alfred permanently. Alfred tells Andre, that his and Ismalia's superior guides recommended that Alfred first rightly learn to appreciate what God has given him and to not thrust it aside so easily. Alfred tells Andre:

> "I am the one who must learn how to elevate myself, and it's for this reason that we haven't had permission to remain together yet. I am paying the right price for my hastiness. Because of my impulsiveness, I lost my inner peace, my home,

> and my wonderful wife. I did not kill, I did not steal, but I feel as if I poisoned myself. Slander is an invisible monster which spreads poison through undiscerning ears and eyes."[119]

Alfred will achieve his goal, with the help of his true love Ismalia. By his hard work and dedication he shall advance in his spiritual quest and be united once again with Ismalia. He is not rushing his rehabilitation; he is calmly building a solid foundation to be a proper partner for his wife.

# Chapter 19 - How to Ascend

Now that you understand what reincarnation is for (your path to perfection), the question is how do you succeed? What should be the governing philosophy of your life that will not only allow you to survive your trials but emerge victorious?

Many religions have told us this before, and of course we try to selectively choose what we wish to follow in order to create that balance between being a good person (in our own minds) and living in the culture that we were born into. We all understand that life is one of constant choices, between good and evil, comfort and hardship, honor and advancement; nothing is totally black and white to us.

Society forces us to compromise daily, the little lies we tell to smooth over difficulties, the moments we advert our gaze away from problems that seem unsurmountable. The times that we have to restrain our secret desires, the times we give in. The spirit world doesn't expect us to be chaste saints. They fully understand the thousand burdens we are exposed to as soon as we take on a physical mantle.

In fact we are expected and even pushed to go out into the world to accomplish two goals. First, to learn how to survive in many different situations from multiple points of view, so we have amassed the experience to fully comprehend every possible combination of life events. To internalize the message from these trials, so that we may be able to extend our love and understanding to others caught in the same circumstances. Whereupon, in our next life we should be able to effectively surmount problems and assist others in their endeavors, with a cool head and a calm heart.

Secondly, if at all possible, we are present to set an example. To help lead society to a kinder, more inclusive state, which shall move our planet a bit closer to the goal of a just world. Most probably, not by any active role, but simply living an honorable life, a pillar to all, where others know you to be impartial and wise; a person to come to for advice and comfort. An example for those around you to follow, in which we must partake fully in our civil duties to show that we are all in this together and we all must provide guidance and solutions. Solutions which are equitable to all and still allow those who need to strive for betterment in their lives to achieve that goal.

## The List

Every religion or doctrine has their list. We have the Ten Commandments, separate rules for Buddhists, Mormons, and countless others. There are similarities and there are differences. The major difference with Spiritism is there are no ceremonial or dietary rules, only moral, because whatever rituals you perform, clothes you wear, or food you consume is unimportant and has no effect on your spiritual condition. If you wish to follow any type of non-moral regulations, that is entirely up to you.

Here is my list, not in any particular order, and this is not the official Spiritist list, I have gathered what I believe to be pertinent from the books by Allan Kardec, Francisco C. Xavier and others Spiritist writers. One other caution, do I practice what I preach? No, I fail constantly. I wrote this more for myself than you, to give me a goal post, anything where I could think back and measure my progress or stagnation. Hence, please discover for yourself what is relevant to you and ignore what you deem unrequired.

1. Love
2. Fraternity
3. Charity
4. Honor
5. Selflessness
6. Spiritualism

Sounds pretty easy, doesn't it? I look at this list and think that I am pretty far along! I am ready for a higher level! But take a second look and decipher what is the opposite of each, for that determines what we can't do.

### Love

The opposite of love is hate. Therefore, don't hate; not even your local corner drug dealer. Don't wish that he or she could be placed on a garbage barge and towed far away to be dumped in the ocean. Don't hate those people who are killing others in YouTube executions. See this is actually pretty tough!

Most of us know, not to hate because of race, sexual preference, religion or any other differences; society has come far. We can intellectualize why it would be wrong. But when we see a specific example our first impulse is to smash it like a bug. Without hesitation and without pity.

Why is that? Because our instinct, created by multiple lifetimes of primitive survival, informs us to remove threats to our life and to our tribe's welfare. After all, wouldn't the vast majority of society be better off without such vermin? The short answer is of course it would! But, that would be the answer if we only had one life and protecting our gene pool is our greatest imperative. The sad fact is that we too have been the equivalent to a worthless piece of scum within society. Hence, we need to pity that person and pray for their enlightenment. This is not to say, they shouldn't be locked up; after all a good decade or so behind bars may give them the suffering required for them is think twice about embarking on the same career in their next life. Who knows, that thug in prison could be a great leader in a thousand years.

Control your hate, you can be indignant, which focuses your energy on solving a problem. But for pure hate, it's a bad habit, so try to break it. Practice when you think about the monsters ruling North Korea, that no matter how good they think they have it, while their populace is terrorized and starving, that they shall wake from their bodies with the realization their actions weren't such a good idea. Through suffering, in the spirit world and in their next physical life, the despotic leaders will understand the wrongness of their approach.

## Fraternity

No problem including everyone into your sphere of assistance and caring, right? Except for that lower class family down the street, or that girl with the piercings that sells coffee. The reverse of fraternity is exclusion. We all do this every day. Every time I walk down the street and pass by beggars on the sidewalk, I exclude the ones that look like drug users or alcoholics and I may give to those who at least have a somewhat decent appearance.

This is a normal human reaction. We find it very challenging to be indiscriminate. Try to think how we too have been on the outside and have needed help. At the very least a polite nod and an accepting smile. The spirit world doesn't expect us to all be Mother Theresa's. But we can be like that statue in the park, looking down at everyone with absolute impartiality; supplying shade to those who choose to sit in our shadow.

## Charity

Miserly comes to mind as the antonym of charity. I hear you saying,"You can't call me miserly because I can't give to charity." Yes, you are right. Most of us just mange to get by and the constant stream of request for money from governments, schools, churches, girl and boy scouts drain whatever is left of our spendable cash. This is where governments work to absolve us of our feeling to be charitable. They take money from us and distribute it to the poor. All laudable, but this robs us of that closeness to helping others and the joy to see the deserving poor gain relief and a little slice of happiness because of our efforts.

You aren't required to give money, only your heart and time is enough. What you give is up to you, be it advice, spiritual help, mowing the lawn for one who can't, whatever will let you feel the accomplishment of performing an altruistic service.

## Honor

Dishonorable, cheat, lie, skim off the top, take more than your share all forms of behavior to avoid. Most people do shun these acts. A vast majority try every day to be fair and honorable in their daily interactions. We have an innate belief in justice. We wish to live in a just society and we realize that without our behavior conforming to that precept, we can't hope to attain our noble goal. Everyone has that feeling. It is the inheritance of the spirit world, where all of God's laws are just. Punishments are meted out, but those are souls descending to the level of their choice and redemption is always waiting for each individual like regular spacing of bus stops. Each time a spirit gets off one ride, they have choices to board the bus to righteousness or stay on the line to sorrow. It's our free will.

So why is honor sometimes difficult to maintain? For those whose goal is to amass wealth at the expense of everything, honor simply isn't part of the equation. But for the rest of us, we are forced to suffer nicks and cuts in our honor shield due to many causes. Just the daily work routine, where the culture is to derive a profit above all else, influences our actions. Flexibility is required given the pressures we are under. We must be careful not to deceive or take advantage of others.

For example, during the internet boom, in the late 1990's, I consulted for a software company that would issue a press release for vaporware (software that doesn't exist), in hopes that it would raise the stock price. Amusingly, soon afterwards another company would issue a press release announcing they had software that could connect to our non-existent software. At one event, where software businesses would gather to speak to Wall Street, I talked to a consultant for a firm that reported they could work with our vaporware. When I told him the truth, he looked at me, and we both laughed and shook our heads. What could we do? Neither of us was in a position to halt such a practice. Therefore, I did what I could, bide my time until I could get another job. Thankfully, I didn't have to look for another position for long, because the lies finally caught up with them and the company went under.

I truly believe that it is harder for a rich person to enter heaven. What I saw during the times when people went wild chasing after that multi-million dollar payoff made an impression. From that time, I understood that if the prize is large enough even basically good people will abandon their principles to grab their pot of gold.

The belief in Spiritism and in the Doctrine that spells out we must pay our debts and reincarnate to learn our lessons effectively removes the quest for ill-gotten gains. Why should we shed our morals and expose our immortal soul for a brief instant of pleasure.

## Selflessness

At first, selflessness may seem to overlap with charity and fraternity, but the opposite is selfishness, which may lead us to discover further situations to avoid.

Emanuel Swedenborg in his book, *Heaven and Hell*, talks about how selfishness leads souls to remain tied to earth and unable to ascend. He marvels at that, since we all must be selfish to some extent, otherwise why would we work, why would we invent, why would we open a business, except to gain rewards. He asks the question, how could selfishness be so bad?

He finds the answer in "Love of self is to wish well to oneself alone, and to others only for the sake of self, even to the church, one's country, or any human society. It consists also in doing good to all these solely for the sake of one's own reputation, honor, and glory; and unless these are seen in the uses he performs in behalf of others he says in his heart, How does this concern me? Why should I do this? What shall I get from it? And therefore does not do it."[120]

The opposite is accomplishing for the accumulation of possessions for the uses of good that can be marshalled for the benefit of others and society. In this case we use our selfishness twofold, one to accumulate credit to allow us the power to guide changes in our life or society to use for good, and the other to use the wealth, or part of it, directly to benefit those who are in need.

Therefore, the question to ask yourself, do you perform acts for only what can be given to you? In your work, do you let others fail, so that you may look better? Do you take credit for another person's idea? I know I have! When I was intent on moving up the corporate ladder and saw the tactics utilized by those at the top, I copied them. I didn't feel good about it, but I consciously acted selfish in a most base manner with the hope that I too could reap rewards. I felt like a shark circling the bait ball, picking off the most naïve and trusting. What a fool I was.

Do yourself a favor and get into the habit of giving credit where credit is due. Help out those who need a boost, even though it may reduce your share of the raise pool at the end of the year. Some enterprises may wish to pit us against each other like fighting dogs, but that doesn't mean we have to play the game.

## Spiritualism

This should be easy! We can all bless others and read more about how to improve. Yes, that is certainly part of the equation. However, as we ponder our spirituality, listening to satellite radio in our leased car, while wearing the latest fashion, do we feel the weight of materialism pulling us down, like gravity, to earth?

The reverse of spiritualism is materialism. This constitutes the age old struggle between focusing our thoughts higher toward our moral qualities or lower toward our immediate desires. Maintaining a balance is difficult. After all, we work hard and deserve a reward. There is nothing wrong with material pleasures as long as they aren't the driving factor of our existence. As an example, you work two jobs to afford that new car, while your kids are left to figure out their homework and problems on their own. This type of behavior may signal that your priorities need to be altered.

Own your possessions, don't let them own you. Know that you can live simply and in the process be stress-free by little acts of denial. There is a whole movement for simpler living currently thriving, full of people who realize that burdening themselves with a mountain of debt really doesn't buy happiness. Just the contrary, it brings worries and anxieties.

If you think you can't cut back because of what your friend

would say, then are they really your friends? If they are your friends, then they don't care more for the latest gadget than you. It is you they want to associate with, and you they wish to be part of their lives.

Instead of shopping, pick up a book or search the internet for information about Spiritism and read it. Learn what is gained by making small changes in your life.

## Keep Learning and Training

The purpose of the list is to guide us to appreciate that by focusing our energies on knowledge and understanding others with love and caring we enable our pure spirit. We lighten the ties that connect us to earth. As we gain wisdom we realize that everything in the physical world evolves into decay. Every building, every statue will one day be dust. One day the earth, the sun and the entire solar system shall be dead planets shrouded in darkness. But you, an immortal soul, shall remain, performing good works on other planets in other universes.

With that knowledge, train yourself to be in the habit to think positive thoughts, to wish all well, bless those unfortunates as you pass them by. Restrain your malicious gossip and concentrate building up others. You may not be recognized in this life, but that is totally unimportant, for you shall be on your way to perfection. And with perfection, you will have the ability to aid others more effectively and to be a difference in the destiny of Earth.

# Chapter 20 – Types of Trials which are not due to Past Wrongs

There are many types of trials that we must experience. Most of our trials on earth are there to pay for our past wrongs, and teach us how the other person felt when we committed the incorrect act, one important point to remember is that besides the trials we are assigned due to our own failings, there are an additional four possible reasons for what we live through here on earth.

1. Random Events

2. Trials that we Request

3. Trials that increase our range of experiences

4. Missions

We may not know what type of lessons we are entertaining at the time, but if we analyze our attitudes and behaviors, we may deduce with high probability the broad category. Let's start with the most common.

## Random Events - Synchronicity

I will be clear up front, some Spiritist believe that none or very close to zero random events occur to us. They believe; there is no such thing as coincidences. Almost every encounter, every event, such as meeting a friend on a street corner by accident, isn't actually an accident. That uncle that called you out of the blue did so for some purpose, which may remain hidden from us forever, or at some time in the future the purpose will be revealed.

There is a word for this; Synchronicity. According to Wikipedia, "Synchronicity is the experience of two or more events as meaningfully related, where they are unlikely to be causally related. The subject sees it as a meaningful coincidence. The concept of synchronicity was first described by Carl Jung, a Swiss psychologist, in the 1920s." [121]

Jung dived deeper into the term, and in fact he saw these random events guided by some higher order, or in his words a "deeper order". He believed that life was not composed of random events, but was laid out for a purpose. There is an orderly framework to our life, which would assist in our intellectual and spiritual growth, "with the purpose of shifting a person's egocentric conscious thinking to greater wholeness."[122]

Below is a diagram illustrating Jung's concept, from the Synchronicity Wikipedia site:

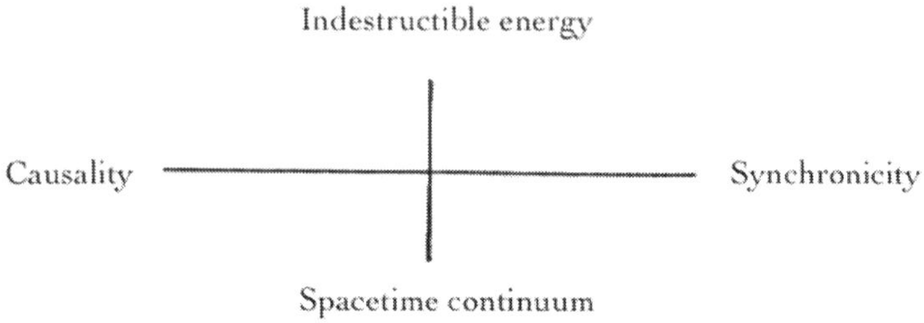


"Shifting a person's egocentric conscious thinking to greater wholeness" could be the definition for the reason for reincarnation. What are we but immature souls on a planet where we reside to learn to be less selfish and more fraternal? Not only was Jung correct about our supposedly unique life, but his theorem could be used to prove the arc of our multiple lives, as we advance from a primitive, brutal animal who takes what he or she can, to a civilized soul, who understands the importance of self-discipline in order to make society function smoothly.

Jung, in his book Synchronicity, supplies us an example:

"My example concerns a young woman patient who, in spite of efforts made on both sides, proved to be psychologically inaccessible. The difficulty lay in the fact that she always knew better about everything. Her excellent education had provided her with a weapon ideally suited to this purpose, namely a highly polished Cartesian rationalism with an impeccably "geometrical" idea of reality. After several fruitless attempts to sweeten her rationalism with a somewhat more human understanding, I had to confine myself to the hope that something unexpected and irrational would turn up, something that would burst the intellectual retort into which she had sealed herself. Well, I was sitting opposite her one day, with my back to the window, listening to her flow of rhetoric. She had had an impressive dream the night before, in which someone had given her a golden scarab — a costly piece of jewelry. While she was still telling me this dream, I heard something behind me gently tapping on the window. I turned round and saw that it was a fairly large flying insect that was knocking against the window-pane from outside in the obvious effort to get into the dark room. This seemed to me very strange. I opened the window immediately and caught the insect in the air as it flew in. It was a scarabaeid beetle, or common rose-chafer (Cetonia aurata), whose gold-green color most nearly resembles that of a golden scarab. I handed the beetle to my patient with the words, "Here is your scarab." This experience punctured the desired hole in her rationalism and broke the ice of her intellectual resistance. The treatment could now be continued with satisfactory results."[123]

In the works of Francisco C. Xavier, the books dictated to "Chico" Xavier by the spirit Andre Luiz, have many examples of how the spirit world influences events. An example from the "deeper order" aka the spirit world, would be the episode when a medium was supposed to go to a meeting so a séance could take place which would assist discarnate spirits. The woman was about to leave the house when her slightly drunk husband returned from his bar hopping early and demanded dinner and for her to stay with him. The spirit team in charge of the mediums meeting quickly influenced the husband's sister to come over to the house, offer to make dinner and to stay with the husband while the medium went to her important meeting. To the medium, it appeared as a coincidence, a lucky break that her sister-in-law decided at that moment to pop over and allowed her to make her appointment.

It wasn't a lucky break; it was an example of a manipulation of events by a power not of this world, belonging to a universe that we do not perceive, but we are part of and ultimately report to. What is the extent of their influence? Do they regulate the flight of each butterfly, which could affect our weather patterns? I don't know the answer and this knowledge may be shielded from us.

All of us can think back and spot a moment when we either needed something at a precise moment and got it by pure chance or tried to do something stupid (looking back at it from a mature point of view) and were prevented by circumstances beyond our control. Was it chance or predetermination? Or when we did a completely idiotic stunt, were we allowed so we could learn the hard way? Did the potential girlfriend or boyfriend we passionately wanted to get acquainted with during college, but could never arrange it; was that the guiding hand of the spirit world, herding us to a more constructive relationship at a later time? Once you start considering the alternate paths we may have travelled and how the unseen hand of destiny opened some doors while closing others, you begin to see the amount of effort and planning that is involved in getting the human race onto the correct road. We are like elementary school children, being actively manipulated, all the while totally clueless, enjoying ourselves, constantly wandering off the planned path, but being gently herded back onto it, all in the hope that we, the little ones, may somehow pick up a useful amount of knowledge.

Therefore, is everything completely planned? I don't think so; I believe there are accidents and coincidences. Randomness still occurs. That bee sting could just be what it is. On the other hand, the overall arc of our life, the trials, the major sufferings, they are prearranged, tracked, and our conduct is reported upon and the results are stored. Welcome to the classroom of life!

### Trials that we request

These are the types of trials that ambitious spirits sign up for in order to advance toward perfection. Good spirits are eager to climb the ladder to excellence. By the way, these are the types who continuously raise their hand in class, or keep asking questions to the teacher, when all you want is to get out of there. Unfortunately, they are also successful in later life, thereby proving that hard work pays off. I detest it when taking the shortcut isn't successful.

Whereas, most understand the need to pay for their accumulated debts, many want to go beyond the cycle of slow growth toward perfection and request more difficult tasks. The type of tasks that are considered are ones that impose a heavy burden, such as devoting your life to helping a disabled brother or sister, thereby sacrificing your happiness in the service of another. To be of service to our fellow souls is a difficult calling. Taking away your options for a fuller life, where it could be the chance to acquire property, love, or the pursuit of your dreams.

Good spirits may also request and be granted an opportunity to help a soul reform. As an example, the prospective parents wanting to be of use to increase the spread of virtue among the human race volunteer for an additional level of difficultly. This type of request is indirectly referred to in *The Spirits Book*:

> *209. How is it that good and virtuous parents often give birth to children of perverse and evil nature? In other words, how is it that the good qualities of the parents do not always attract to them, through sympathy, a good spirit to animate their child?*
>
> "A wicked spirit may ask to be allowed to have virtuous parents, in the hope that their counsels may help him to amend his ways; and God often confides such an one to the care of virtuous persons, in order that he may be benefited by their affection and care."[124]

How many of us have seen wonderful families, with good parents, had that lone black sheep. We look at the family situation in wonder and attempt to analyze how that child could be so different from the others. The answer is that even with the best of intentions, reforming an errant spirit is a daunting task. Blessed are those who step forward and demonstrate their dedication to assist needy souls.

As covered before in the topic on childhood and reincarnation, a child is malleable until their true character becomes apparent, usually in the middle or late teens. Hence, we see small children, under the influence of their parents, behaving dutifully, and then a transformation occurs, where their past lives intrude on their behavior, for their conscience and instincts have been reinforced in the wrong direction. If they had retained the force of will to fervently wish to grow toward the good, these children are able to surmount their past. If not, they will leave a path of sadness and destruction among their parents, brothers and sisters. Whatever the outcome, the parents will be rewarded for their intent.

I hesitate to use the terms debit and credit, because it implies an impersonal ledger, where one must carefully weigh the good that we do, our credits, with the wrongs we commit, our debits, and hope that we come out with a positive balance at the end of each life. For this doesn't measure the amount of our love, the expansion of our attitude to be forgiving and helpful to all, the holistic growth that our soul may have experienced. Nor does it peer into the extent of our selfishness, our love for our possessions that may have ruled us. Outwardly seeming to be at peace with the world, but in reality loving our goods more than our family.

At the end of the day, we still must sum up the positive and negative to arrive at the distance that we have gained. Overcoming obstacles, contributing to others or societies well-being insures that we have a positive mark for our ledger. Hence, from a purely accounting view, taking on more is logical. Whereas, the amassing of credit is familiar to us, the spirit world sees this differently. We shouldn't underestimate their desire to be of service. The love that is showered upon us springs from their hearts. We need to always be aware that they too have walked in our shoes. They have felt the pain and the confusion that comes with a physical body.

Socrates said that no human can ever know wisdom while locked in a container with a thousand distractions. The best that we can do is find temporary haven in our studies and meditations, feeling those moments of bliss when we are detached and can concentrate on our progress. Outside of that, we must soldier on, performing what we can, maintaining a good attitude. After all, this is but an instant of time in your immortal life.

When you see the social worker helping the dispossessed, your friend that is trapped providing constant care for a relative, the reverend or priest who walks among the deserving poor, please realize these are altruistic souls who will not only serve those in the here and now, but shall be a force for good for many lives in the future.

## Rounding out our Training

Sorry, we aren't allowed to fly through a good life and graduate with honors. No matter how saint-like we behave in one life, we are still required to accumulate an impressive set of proficiencies. As discussed earlier, to become an effective high level spirit we need to be forged in real-life events. Some are educational, some are painful, and others are a nuisance. All are meant to expose us to varied sections of life.

Pure spirits are powerful entities, who are able to travel instantaneously by thought and manifest themselves in varied levels of matter and appearance. One would not want these uber-souls to lack the training required. An effective army is measured by their reaction to every circumstance. The reactions are not mere collective happenstance, but brought about by repetitive drilling and participation in real life scenarios.

Want to know what to do during a peasant revolt? Then you have to spend time as a peasant. Helping soldiers cope with the stress of battle; then you need to have lived through the hard times as a soldier, and most probably felt the end of your life as you were beaten in combat by an adversary. Need to influence a prestigious leader; then you too should have lived through a time of critical events, where only you were capable of making life and death decisions to insure your community survived and prospered.

Do all of us need to live through every permutation and combination of events? I doubt it, but then we are immortal, so big numbers shouldn't scare us. At the very least, we should be aware of the different points of view, the motivations, the wants and desires, the anxieties and the passions of people from every segment of society.

Only by living in their shoes feeling the hunger or fear they do, can we begin to comprehend the depth of their feelings. Only from that standpoint, could we begin the long process to guide them to a better road. A road which may take lifetimes to find.

Without the viewpoint on high of the trajectories a life must journey, how could we guide the immature spirit in a succession of lives to expose that soul to the required events to evoke a change of heart. To be a leader requires decisions, judgments which may progress or retard a valuable spirit's quest for perfection.

Where I am leading with this? Here; when you ask yourself during those exasperating times, why in the heck do I have to go through this? Now you know one of the possibilities. It could be a valuable stepping stone, or more aptly, one more brick in your foundation to supply you with the fortified structure to build your future upon. You have acquired a valuable data point, a reference, which at some future occasion may prove to be a key to your success. Every event adds to your instincts. Remember, that when you are reborn, your instincts are available for you to utilize.

It's not only with age do we get wiser, but with each new birth, after we are finished with childhood, our conscience and instincts kick in. If you are able to grow in each life, then in the next life, your early adulthood won't be a missing decade of bad decisions. You will be able to build upon your past, insuring a smoother road to success, as opposed to the constant struggle to make something of yourself. You shall have more time to gain more awareness, devote yourself to charity, become more spiritual and survive your trials with élan, instead of complaining at every step.

Does this seem impossible? Haven't we all looked with envy at that young woman or man, who remains calm and composed in every circumstance? Who, by their actions, gain the notice of powerful people, who then target these mature spirits for advancement in positions of power and influence. When, these young enterprising people move into their thirties, they are ready for a career of distinction and substance for decades. Ready to make a difference in society and in many lives.

## Missions

"I am on a mission from God", to quote Elwood from the movie "The Blues Brothers", and most probably many other films and novels, all used in varying degrees, as a comedic line, a reason cited by a fanatic, or from a divine spirit. Wouldn't most of us love to say that line with certainty? With meaning? We all have a longing to be part of a movement larger than ourselves. We spend time, day dreaming of making a contribution to the world, wishing to make a difference. Well, we are here to make a difference, while it may be small imperceptible increments; we still are able to contribute to society's progress, if only by our example.

The spirit world does send members to earth, in the hope that they will be valuable contributors to our progress. Missions are referred to in Allan Kardec's *The Spirits Book*:

> *572. Is a spirit's mission imposed upon him, or does it depend on his own will?*
>
> "He asks for it, and is rejoiced to obtain it."
>
> -- May the same mission be demanded by several spirits?
>
> "Yes, there are often several candidates for the same mission, but they are not all accepted."
>
> *573. In what does the mission of incarnated spirits consists?*
>
> "In instructing men, and aiding their advancement; and in ameliorating their institutions by direct, material means. These missions are more or less general and important; but he who tills the ground accomplishes a mission as really as he who governs or instructs. Everything in nature is linked together; and each spirit, while purifying himself by his incarnation, concurs, under the human form, to the accomplishment of the Providential plans. Each of you has a mission, because each of you can be useful in some way or other."[125]

"Accomplishment of Providential plans", in other words a mission from God. Missions with a direct purpose. There is a starting point, milestones in-between, and an end state. Not just some amorphous statement, such as peace on earth, which is so general, although well meaning, but as a tactical plan, worthless.

Are spirits sent on missions and then forgotten, like throwing a fish back into the water after catching them and forgetting they existed in seconds? No, like any organization that has goals, there is a department, composed of resources committed to the attainment of the objectives. No successful company or government makes a statement or dispatches a person on a task and then supplies no support, no management, no analytics and no reward.

Hence, whenever one of us is sent on a mission, we are not alone. We have been trained and prepared. We may not know consciously that we are meant to accomplish a certain task, but we shall be guided, with spirit hands, and possibly by other physical team members to our aim.

All the while, there must be a support team, monitoring our progress, creating reports and determining modifications to the original plan. At times, we may seem to be solitary, but in reality we are never alone. Spirits on a mission must be scrutinized at every step for hints of failure or unexpected success. New opportunities could present themselves which could be advantageous to pursue.

Are spirits who incarnate and perform missions infallible? Certainly not, for the simple fact that as soon as a spirit merges with a physical body, all actions become massively more difficult, for instead of preparing in a controlled environment, we are now on the battlefield, with a multitude of distractions. Yes, spirits fail, and it is referenced in *The Spirits Guide*:

*578. May spirit fail in his mission through his own fault?*

"Yes; if he is not of a high degree of elevation."

*-- What, for him, are the consequences of such a failure?*

"He is obliged to begin his task over again; this is his punishment. And, besides, he will have to undergo the consequences of the mischiefs caused by his failure."[126]

There must be many failures, for we are a very frail vessel. Take comfort that we are never given tasks that are beyond our ability. Plus, as the difficultly of a mission increases, so does the support. While on a mission, there may be a team of incarnates and discarnates, with additional help from high-order spirits. Therefore, missions don't fail because of a lack of backing; they collapse because of the failure of our will.

Whenever we choose a dubious quick and easy monetary reward over the long and honest road or if we let our passions overrule the sound advice from our conscience, these are the points of failure. A spirit wouldn't be charged with a mission that couldn't be accomplished.

What occurs is that in response to emotions or events we stop listening to our conscience, that valuable voice inside your head, and attempt to find an erroneous way out of our predicament.

Is this easy? Of course not, for I am absolutely certain I have failed many times. Always weakening at a vital point, searching for the fastest escape route. Giving into the current morals of society or following bad advice and doing the wrong thing because everyone else is. Or worse, worshipping that material good or the chance of power at the expense of my moral health; how could I have been so stupid? Easy, I am human.

Blessedly, with every failure comes experience, valuable reconnoitering, so at the next time when approaching that fulcrum, the right path will be determined. The beautiful aspect of being immortal is that you have an eternity to improve. Like the combat video games of today, you can be shot, knifed, drowned or your body parts scattered across the plains, it doesn't matter, you can still just pick yourself up and get back into the game.

Even with some failures, there are small victories. While the end goal may not have been attained, a few positives will appear.

For instance, those on a mission to raise an errant spirit, may not totally reform that poor soul, but they may have nudged their progress a notch or two. *The Spirits Book* mentions this type of trial and its probable outcome:

> *583. If a child goes wrong, notwithstanding the care of his parents, are they responsible?*
>
> "No; but the more vicious the disposition of the child, and the heavier their task, the greater will be their reward if they succeed in drawing him away from the evil road."[127]

As stated in the beginning of this section, in one respect, we are all on a mission. Our primary duty is to prepare ourselves. Believe, for those who are sincere, you are supported and if you ask for guidance, you will receive it.

Examine the popularity of people reporting their NDE's (Near Death Experience), what are the recurring themes? The feeling of love, the review of their life, and lastly the acknowledgement that there is a higher power, are constantly reported.

Upon recovery, most have a greater appreciation of their place in this world, an understanding that we are here to help ourselves, as well as others, find their spiritual goal. Is all this by accident? No, the reports of NDE's are similar from around the world and in different cultures, therefore it must be planned.

Each person who has had the experience was targeted as a potential recruit that could use one more push to attain the necessary credentials to ascend. Each person who discovers the universe of love awaiting them becomes one more spirit who could assist others to make the same journey. By this simple process of rebirth, growth, rebirth, the numbers grow, so that one day we shall live on a world of love, beauty, truth and justice.

# Chapter 21 – Interlude 5 - Beggar Woman – found by Prince Galetzin

In Leon Denis' book, *Life and Destiny*, he relates different stories about reincarnations. In one intriguing anecdote, which occurred in the summer of 1862, he tells us that Prince Galetzin and Count R were together in Hamburg:

> "One evening during a stroll they found a poor woman lying on a bench. Finding she was hungry and penniless, they took her to the hotel and fed her. After she had satisfied a ravenous appetite, the Prince, who possessed magnetic powers (meaning he knew how to hypnotize people), desired to experiment with her." [128]

The woman was put into a trance. Whereas, when they found her, she only spoke a poor, uneducated version of German, she began to speak in perfect French. She told the Prince and the Count, that she was living her present life due to a terrible crime she committed in a past life.

This statement fits perfectly with the Doctrine of Spiritism. If we commit a wrong, it must be paid in the present or a future life. This woman must have perpetrated a major crime to be part of such a difficult trial.

After more questioning, the Prince found out:

> "She lived in a chateau in Brittany on the border of the sea. Having a lover, she desired to be rid of her husband, and pushed him over a precipice into the sea. She described the crime and place minutely; and thanks to this description, Prince Galetzin and Count R later went to Brittany separately, and each made inquiries and investigation with identically the same results. After careful questioning of many people, they found some old peasants who had been told by their parents that history of a beautiful woman who had thrown her husband into the sea."[129]

Later, the Prince visited the Chief of Police of Hamburg and found out the woman was uneducated, spoke a poor version of German, and lived the life of a common beggar.

Again, according to how the process of reincarnation operates, not remembering the past, while you are in your physical body is a requirement. How else will you learn what has been assigned to you? If you had complete memories, you would not give the current situation your full attention; you would know this is a passing moment. But, in the middle of a life, where you believe that you are only here one time, each trial seems to be a dramatic event. Only by this, do you modify your inner-most attitudes and retain that which you have been tasked to absorb.

# Chapter 22 - Trials of the Rich

You may not believe this, but the rich have the most difficult trials. If our growth as a spirit depends on our making the correct choices, then for the wealthy, there is a magnitude more decisions that must be made. For with wealth, comes options. This point becomes clear in the answer to the question, in *The Spirits Book*, about the gauntlet of temptations that we must experience:

> *261. Is it necessary for the spirit, in the course of the trials to which he has to submit in order to arrive at perfection, to undergo every sort of temptation? Must he encounter all the circumstances that can excite in him pride, jealousy, avarice, sensuality, etc.?*
>
> "Certainly not, since there are, as you know, many spirits who take from the beginning a road which spares them the necessity of undergoing many of those trials; but he who suffers himself to be drawn into the wrong road, exposes himself to all the dangers of that road. A spirit, for instance, may ask for riches, and his demand may be granted; and, in that case, he will become, according to his character, avaricious or prodigal, selfish or generous, and will make a noble use of his wealth, or waste it on vanity or sensuality; but this does not imply that he will be compelled to run the gauntlet of all the evil tendencies that may be fostered by the possession of riches."[130]

Notice, when temptations are mentioned, the spirits use the life of riches as an example of multiple enticements. For with wealth comes a horde of people, all ready to give you what you want, no questions asked. Opportunities arise for corruption because the payoff is significant for those who are attempting to gain leverage. There is more discussion about wealth as a trial in Allan Kardec's book, *The Gospel According to Spiritism*:

> "Undoubtedly, wealth is a very slippery trial, more dangerous than poverty because of its allure, the temptations it creates and the fascination it exerts. It is the supreme arouser of pride, selfishness and lust. It is the strongest tie that keeps humans

> bound to the earth and diverts their thoughts from heaven. It produces such giddiness that we often see that those who go from poverty to wealth soon forget their former condition, those who shared with them in it and those who helped them in it, and they become insensitive, selfish and vain. However, even though wealth makes the journey difficult, it does not follow that it makes it impossible or that it cannot become a means of salvation in the hands of those who know how to use it, just as certain poisons can restore health if used purposefully and carefully."[131]

"Supreme arouser of pride, selfishness and lust" is the money quote. Such a base truth. When the riches come pouring in, you want more. Those who honestly gain feel satisfaction, while those who profit by deceit may feel a slight moral twitch, but it is quickly suppressed. Those in the large financial institutions who participate in the selling of goods packaged for the express purpose of unloading dubious monetary instruments on unsuspecting and trusting people know well these emotions.

If you feel at all ashamed at your actions in your pursuit of wealth, that is your conscience talking to you. You certainly have free will to ignore that advice. Just be aware that if you doubt your actions for a reason; because it is morally wrong and you shall pay a price.

### What to do with your Wealth

Now that you are wealthy, and aware of the downsides, what are you supposed to do with it? In the *Gospel According to Spiritism*, you are told exactly what you should be doing:

> "The truth of the matter is that humans have the mission of laboring for the material improvement of the planet; they must reclaim it, cleanse it and make it suitable to someday receive the entire population that its range can bear. In order to feed this ever increasing population, production must be increased. If one country's production is insufficient, it will have to be sought elsewhere. For this very reason, relations between nations become a necessity. In order to facilitate such relations,

it is necessary to destroy physical barriers that separate nations and render communication more rapid. For such endeavors – which are the work of centuries – humans have had to extract materials from the bowels of the earth; they have sought in science the means to execute their endeavors more safely and rapidly. However, to accomplish them, resources are needed; necessity drove humans to create wealth, just as it drove them to discover science. The activity required by these endeavors has increased and developed their intelligence, and this intelligence, which they have concentrated primarily on satisfying their material needs, will help them later on to understand the great moral truths. Since wealth is the primary means of executing these tasks, without it there would be no more great endeavors, no more activity, no stimulus and no research. It is with good reason therefore that wealth is considered an element of progress."[132]

The advice above is completely in-line with what any prudent investor would consider. Money invested in enterprises which provide a benefit to society bring the best surety of outcome. There are other hints in the paragraph above. First, given that the *Gospel According to Spiritism*, was published in 1868, the statement that we must "cleanse" the earth, sounds perfectly reasonable to our ears, but at a time when the industrial revolution was just beginning and environmentalism was unheard of, what was written is relevant today. This is a good illustration of the timeless aspect of Allan Kardec's books. One can read the vast majority of Allan Kardec's five books and not determine the time period in which they were written. Although, I have read one section about dueling!

Secondly, the statement to "render communication more rapid", has been partially accomplished, first by the telegraph and telephone for more than 100 years, but only within the last 20 years has the revolution truly permeated throughout the masses of all countries and all classes. All has been accomplished via the aggregation of wealth, via our capitalistic system and its associated rewards for risking capital.

Therefore, capitalism isn't evil, while there may be scoundrels using it for their unfair gain, the free transfer and accumulation of assets to fund worthy projects are vital to the earth's future. Leaving all decisions in the hand of a few government functionaries, as in the failed communist states, has proven to be a less efficient method of advancement.

### Your wealth and you

OK, so now you know the market or other jobs building enterprises are worthy places to invest, but what about your reward? After all, you worked hard and should enjoy some of the perks? Yes, you should and I have not seen anything written where you shouldn't enjoy that large house, new car, or the latest fashions, if you can afford them. Hence, utilizing your wealth for your own comfort is a just reward for hard work and shepherding your assets for societies gain.

The question is how do you use them? Did you buy that car to show your advantage over a friend? Are you afraid that if you don't own at least three cars others will think you are poor? Do you drive around feeling superior to everyone else? All good activities to get out of the habit of doing.

The difficult part is maintaining your humility and respect for others. What many people do not realize is that a wealthy person is constantly being attacked, not physically, but monetarily, by persons or organizations that are trying to siphon off money. This leads to a wall between the affluent and others, and a defensiveness that may come off as rudeness. All this may lead to a less kind and polite approach to persons around you and in your control. Be careful to treat all with respect, for people tend to be insecure around those wealthier than them.

Know that those who are trying to manipulate your money out of you will get their day of judgment. Eventually, those who tried to take advantage will learn the error of their ways. While the majority, who are sincere and hardworking, deserve respect and guidance from those who are better off.

## The Transmission of Wealth

The question many ask, is since wealth is given to me as a trial, do I have a right to pass it on? The answer is yes and the reasons are covered in *The Gospel According to Spiritism*:

> *15. Does the principle according to which humans are only trustees of the wealth that God has allowed them to enjoy during their lives take away their right to transfer it to their descendants?*
>
> After their death, people can rightly transfer what they have enjoyed during their lives, because the effect of such right is always dependent on the will of God, who can prevent their descendants from enjoying it whenever he wants. That is why we see apparently solidly established fortunes crumble. The will of persons to keep their wealth in the hands of their descendants is therefore powerless, although this fact does not take away their right to transfer the loan they have received, since God will take it from their descendants if he deems it appropriate. St. Louis (Paris, 1868)"[133]

For those of you, who are rich, consider yourselves challenged. You have been given a complex trial, a trial that can be successively completed, but will take an extraordinary sense of patience and noblesse oblige. Noblesse oblige isn't a word you see often anymore, it means the inferred responsibility of privileged people to act with generosity and nobility toward those less privileged, but it is an attitude that is often lacking in today's nouveau riche, who often believes that with wealth comes an automatic sense of superiority and entitlement. Try to fight this inclination and ground yourself in the humility found in the examples of among others, Socrates, Confucius, Buddha and Jesus.

# Chapter 23 – Trials of the Poor

If you are one of those hardworking, honest and humble persons who watches carefully what they spend and deals with the world as you would want them to deal with you; bless you! For you are proceeding through your life as you had intended, your plan is working. In addition, if you are able to instill in your family a notion of God and the spiritual duty of all, then you are learning the lessons that you desired.

The trials of the poor are usually one of unfulfilled dreams and ambitions, coupled with constant self-denial of material goods they are craving. The stories of real people described in Spiritist literature are full of the theme of a rich or powerful figure returning in the next life as a humble worker or worse, a homeless beggar. Emmanuel, the spirit guide of Francisco C. Xavier, himself was a powerful Roman Senator, who actually meets Jesus and rejected his offer to join his revolution of peace. In Emmanuel's next life, he comes back as a slave, who dies in the circus, as a Christian devoured by lions.

Such are the trials of the poor. Glamour is noticeably lacking and the daily grind is on display. Day after day of making ends meet is the repetitive message taught. Most probably interspersed with small tragedies and disappointments and hopefully opportunities to succeed and celebrate. Those who know to value the life they are given, discover ways for them and their families to achieve happiness in their life by finding the value in the little things, such as family time together, playing with the children, spiritual discussions, and other simple pleasures. The lesson is one of humbleness and understanding of those less fortunate. Coupled with the knowledge of the effort it takes to pull yourself up without the step ladder of a more prosperous upbringing.

The Spirits Book talks about the choice of trials and the choices we must make during our sojourn here on earth:

*259. If the spirit has the choice of the kind of trials which he will undergo, does it follow that all the tribulations we experience in the earthly life have been foreseen and chosen by us?*

"It would not be correct to say that such has been the case with all of them; for you cannot be said to have chosen and foreseen all the things which happen to you in this life, and all their details. You have chosen the kind of trial to which you are subjected; the details of this trial are a consequence of the general situation which you have chosen, and are often the result of your own actions."

"If, for instance, a spirit has chosen to be born among malefactors, he knew to what kind of temptations he was exposing himself, but not each one of the actions which he would accomplish; those actions are the effect of his volition, of his free-will. A spirit knows that, in choosing such and such a road, he will have such and such a kind of struggle to undergo; he knows, therefore, the nature of the vicissitudes which he will encounter, but he does not know whether these will present themselves under one form or under another. The details of events spring from circumstances and the force of things. It is only the leading events of his new life, those which will exercise a determining effect on his destiny, that are foreseen by him. If you enter upon a road full of ruts, you know that you must walk very warily, because you run a risk of stumbling; but you do not know the exact place where you will stumble, and it may be that, if you are sufficiently on your guard, you will not stumble at all. If, when you are passing along a street, a tile falls upon your head, you must not suppose that 'it was written,' as the common saying is."[134]

Hence, not all events are predetermined, depending on the path we chose and the decisions we make, the road may be smoother or rougher. With the trials of the poor, the effects of events may be harder to glide over, for the lack of money tends to make life more difficult and responses more limited.

## Trials of the Underclass

There are also trials where a person is not only born into

poverty, but also in the underclass. Where he or she will expect to be immersed in criminal enterprises. Truly this would be an exceptionally challenging trial, demanding great character to resist the lure and pressures of the immediate family. *The Spirit's Book* tells us why this would transpire:

> *260. How can a spirit choose to be born among those who are leading a bad life?*
>
> "It is necessary for him to be sent into the conditions which will furnish the elements of the trial he has demanded. To this end, there must be a correspondence between the imperfection of which he desires to free himself, and the social surroundings into which he is born. For example, if he has to struggle against the instinct of brigandage, it is necessary for him to be thrown among brigands."[135]

It would be tough to come up with a harder task than this. Although, I am sure, there have been many who were successful. For instance, one reads report about Roma who have successfully sought an education and escaped the stereotypical gypsy life of petty theft and con games. It is a testament to the character of those spirits who ask and triumph in such dire circumstances.

## Trial of Envy

When you have only what you require to survive, the urge to be jealous of others with visible signs of prosperity is immense. People connect possessions with happiness and believe, like a child believes, that only if they could get that one object, they would feel better. Yes, the pleasure may last for a bit, but in the long run you are left with yourself. It is your attitude that enables one to feel pleasure in life's little moments, not objects. Besides, don't be fooled by the seemingly happy façade of the better off, as is articulated in *The Gospel According to Spiritism*; the spirit Lacordaire, writes in 1863, about the sad thoughts of a poor young woman:

> "You would love to adorn your head with flowers and mingle with the wealthy of this earth. You say to yourself that, like

> these women who pass you by, nonchalant and laughing, you too could be rich. Oh! Be still, child! If you knew how many tears and nameless sorrows are hidden beneath those embroidered dresses, how many sobs are muffled under the noise of that joyous orchestra, you would prefer your humble solitude and your poverty."[136]

Modern poverty in the western world brings about another sort of envy. Whereas in Europe and America the poor class is provided with the basics required for daily life, in many instances, no other demand from their part is made. Hence, these suffering souls are left idle, watching our media beam propaganda to them, convincing them they are missing out on the latest gadgets. Thereby, causing immense jealously amongst the poor and idle class.

This type of social dysfunction is what causes riots, like the one in London, where the youth looted, not grocery stores to gain food for their families, but shoe stores and others like them that contained the latest fashions, so they too could wear what is popular.

These spirits who are on earth to learn the dignity of a day of hard work are being done a disservice by society. The spirit world doesn't encourage idleness, far from it; dedication and the pursuit of knowledge are the qualities they want us to absorb. On one occasion, when Francisco C. Xavier, the most famous medium and Spiritist in Brazil was asked if he wanted to tell the people of Brazil anything, he said in essence, work hard and don't complain.

# Chapter 24 – Trials of the Middle Class

The spirit world promoted the rise and spread of Western Civilization for many reasons, but one of them was the creation of the middle class. Those warriors, who willingly show up to work every day, fulfill their tasks, attempting to live a decent life, not complaining and contributing their all, treating each other honestly and participating in the civil and spiritual lives of their community is a significant example presented to us by the spirit world. Why is this important? Because this is the future. When humanity is a collection of more good than evil, social divisions will gradually fade. Leaders will be in their position for merit only and nations will be at peace. We shall all be middle class.

Middle class life is a reflection of life in the heavenly cities, it may be at times a poor reflection, but at its core, a society that goes about its business, tackling problems, serving those who require it, growing toward scientific, philosophy, and religious advancements is the goal. All eternal values that spirits who wish to rise to perfection must strive for. Perfected spirits are elements that exist to help others become perfected. Therefore we must transform ourselves into vehicles for dedicated service. No, not a life of dreary paper pushing, but an exciting career of discovery and the pursuit of knowledge. Where, at the day's end we feel we have made a difference, not just a dollar.

Because you may be born middle class, still doesn't protect you from the trials you must suffer to repair any damages from your past lives. Hence, you may experience, disease, divorce, poverty due to unforeseen circumstances, etc. All of the vicissitudes that life can deliver to you and in which you are expected to learn the lessons presented.

### Living for Work, Not Work for a Living

What are the advantages and disadvantages of being middle class? The disadvantages are, to many of us in this present position, numerous and most of them have to do with the need to live hand to mouth. Not in the same manner of those poor people who utilize the weekly paycheck loan establishment that robs them with enormous interest rates. But in the sense that we are not able to stop working. Yes, we could survive on our assets for a while between jobs, but we would be forced to look for gainful employment during the time of idleness. Which as any unemployed person knows, is not idleness, but a daily struggle to procure new work. Where we must strive hard to motivate ourselves to keep up the search and maintain a good attitude in the face of repetitive and sometimes downright ignorant questions from prospective employers.

We find ourselves on the outside looking in and longing to be part of a group that securely enables us to work and regain self-pride. For isn't this the crux of the middle class life, we measure our stature by what we do, not by who we are. The two are intertwined in our minds and the minds of others.

We are constantly told, we should focus on us the person, not what we accomplish or not accomplish, but on our character and our self-worth. True, we do need to be introspective and correctly gauge who we are and what we need to improve upon. Unfortunately, this isn't enough for the spirit world.

Therefore, the disadvantage of having to work for a living is actually an advantage. Would you train combat soldiers for battle by having them sit around on a couch watching TV? How would they perform when first thrust into battle? Most likely, retreat as humanly possible, for they had never known the discipline required to survive and triumph under fire.

How well will you be prepared for life in the spirit world? Do you think they sit around all day contemplating beauty? No, the higher level of the spirit world, those above the earth, the heavenly cities are beehives of activity. One can't visualize the amount of effort put forth to guide us by the spirit world. We are similar to pre-school children who constantly need to be watched or they would do something self-destructive.

The types of work found in the higher planes are beyond our imagination. One aspect is certain; everyone will find a passion for something. A career where the work is the reward. Where every day is another challenge to be met and a joy to partake, one in which your intellect is stimulated and your desires are rewarded.

You may ask, this isn't the case here on earth, I have to work in a nine to five job, which I force myself to wake up every morning to go fulfill my duty. There are two responses to this state of affairs. First, through your choices, you selected the type of career you are now in. Quite logically, you probably insured that your choice was able to provide you with a decent living. A decent living meaning the minimum level in which you wished to live your life. There may have been other choices that were your passion, but you knew choices would have to be made in order to live within your means if you embarked on the other path. Again, the decision to sacrifice your passion for better material living was yours.

As you ascend in the spiritual hierarchy, the material restraints are loosened, and the lure of your living your calling is stronger. You will be more than comfortable with sacrificing monetary gain for intellectual stimulation. We see this all attitude all of the time. Teachers who work with children, knowing they will never drive a new car. Social workers helping others, giving up living in the neighborhood they were raised, in order that others may have a path for a successful life. Artists and writers living in dire poverty, so they could pursue their dreams.

The second response to the question of why you are locked in a unfulfilling career is that take heart; you are learning the routine of contributing every day. You are training for the afterlife, where participating in constructive activity on a regular basis is expected and the only method of advancement. The added bonus is that now, you shall be able to follow your passion and decide your mode of study. Plus, the greater the breadth of experience, the wider the choices of tasks.

## Temptations of the Middle Class

As in any life here on earth, temptations are as numerous as the number of people around us. There are always "friends" ready to lead us into all sorts of trouble. Whither it could be excessive drinking, drugs, questionable adventures, vicious gossip, or other actions that are not conducive to our well-being. All that needs to be said is to follow your conscience, that device which has untold number of centuries of experience under its belt. Listen for the voice that says you have gone too far or stop immediately. Then heed it and make a course correction.

For it is this type of self-destructive behavior that usually precedes a fall from a middle or higher class existence. Where the effect of a self-destructive habit slowly breaks down your innate moral character and shuts off the pathway for you to correctly heed the warnings of your own soul.

Where does our weakness originate when we allow ourselves to fall behind in our lessons? There are numerous causes, but boredom, is the great virus of destruction for many of us. When bored, we seek stimulation, any outside influence to carry us out of our current routine. We become bored because we are constantly bombarded by propaganda telling us we should be doing something else. Doing anything that entails spending money to purchase a good or a service. Commercials that demonstrate, via TV, internet, and billboards, hour after hour that only through the purchase of an item, that our life will be improved.

When we lack the means to buy ourselves out of our predicament, we take the less expensive way out and alter our minds through artificial methods. The better decision would be to meditate upon our life and determine why we are at a moment where we have nothing fulfilling to perform. The best answer is to discover spiritual work, for ourselves or others. For in this materialistic culture that we reside in, we need to fight to balance our ties to the physical world with our real connections to the spiritual world, where the majority of our existence will occur.

In conclusion, to be able to survive and thrive in a middle class environment is a blessing not a curse. For via our immersion into a class of society that encourages honesty and justice, combined with hard work and a civic obligation is valuable training to impart habits that will take us forward in good standing when we pass over to the spirit world.

# Chapter 25 – Interlude 6 – Two Lives – Souria-Omar and Epaminondas de Vigo

## Souria-Omar

In the book, *Memoirs of a Suicide*, a group of recovering suicides are being introduced to their mentors, who will help them prepare for their next reincarnation. One mentor is introduced and a compilation of his previous lives is given:

> "On my left is Souria-Omar, an ancient master of initiation in Alexandria, and then a philosopher in Greece, right after the coming of Socrates, when undying torch-lights began to be lit for the people, until then deprived of the sublime knowledge, which was kept secret and available only for learning and use by sages and scholars. Like the eminent precursor (meaning Socrates, who preceded Christ) of the Great Master, he taught the Secret Doctrine to disciples coming from the humblest social classes, to the disinherited and the unfortunate. In the benevolent shade of stately oak trees or the poetic amenity of the plantains, he enabled then to absorb teachings filled with divine magnificence, transporting then to lofty thoughts about the eternal God, Creator of all things, that unknown God whose image was absent from the collection of deities on the stone altars of ancient Hellas… Later, he reincarnated in Judea, attracted by the figure of the incomparable Master of masters, practicing benevolent, humble acts as he followed the luminous footsteps of the heavenly Shepard! In old age, he witness the Jerusalem persecution right after the stoning of Stephen. Stoic, strengthened by an unbreakable faith, he suffered a long martyrdom in the sinister darkness of an ancient dungeon; afflicted by blindness, he had been considered to be a learned person, and therefore dangerous to Pharisaic interests. Tortured with beating and dreadful mutilations , he succumbed, ignored by society and unacknowledged by his own family, but glorified by the Sublime Master for whose love he endured everything with humility, love and gratitude."[137]

One can only stand in awe of spirits like Souria-Omar. I have no doubt, that if I were tortured, I would quickly renounce whatever they wanted me to and adopt the state religion like a fanatic!

## Epaminondas de Vigo

Again in the book, *Memoirs of a Suicide*, another mentor is introduced:

> "On my right is Epaminondas de Vigo, who in a brilliant ascent from ancient Egypt to the somber days of the Middle Ages in Spain, always served the Truth and praised the name of God. His triumph has not diminished one bit in the spirit realms. In apostolic times, when as a disciple of Simon Peter he glorified the Divine Master, he had the supreme honor of being martyred in the circus of Domitius Nero. In Spain, under the empire of darkness that enveloped the laws imposed by the so-called Holy Office of the Inquisition, he shone like a saving star, showing sublime pathways to the persecuted, as well as to many other hearts longing for the divine ideal, bearing the torch of knowledge sublimated in love and reverence for the Gospel of the Immaculate Lamb, knowledge he had obtained in past pilgrimages devoted to the sacred wisdom of India, the learned repository of immortal truths on the earth! But it was exactly because he did shine in the darkness that he was martyred once more, not by having his physical body thrown to the lions, but by having it burned at the stake, where he once more proved his unflinching devotion to Jesus of Nazareth!"[138]

Doesn't that make you feel totally inconsequential? I am sure if I had to create my resume of past lives; I would appear as, at best, a behind-kissing sycophant, always bending to the latest fad in the hope of material advancement.

I kept the hardest examples until last. We could only hope to aspire to just a portion of these beautiful souls. But, if we always keep honesty and justice in the forefront of our minds, all of us, will someday reach the same level of goodness.

# Chapter 26 - Suicide - An Undesirable Method to escape your Trial

We Spiritists are taught that we must pay in this life or the next for the wrongs we have committed. But for suicide, the payment is immediate. In Andre Luiz's first book, *Nosso Lar*, psychographed by Francisco C. Xavier, published in 1944, Andre dies and is sent to:

> "Actually, I felt like a prisoner trapped behind dark bars of horror. With my hair on end, my heart pounding, and scared stiff, I often cried out like a madman. I begged for mercy and clamored against the painful despondency that had taken hold of my spirit. But when my loud cries didn't fall on an implacable silence, they were answered by lamenting voices even more pitiful than my own. At other times, sinister laughter rent the prevailing silence. I thought that some unknown companion out there was a prisoner of insanity. Diabolical forms, ghastly faces, animal-like countenances appeared from time to time, increasing my panic. When it wasn't pitch dark, the landscape seemed to be bathed in a lurid light as if shrouded in a thick mist that was warmed from afar by the rays of the sun."[139]

Sounds horrible. Andre told of people coming to him and calling out "Suicide!", but he knew he didn't commit suicide. It wasn't until he was rescued by the spirits from Nosso Lar, that he discovered that he was a suicide, an "unconscious suicide", which denotes that he drank and whored himself to death (or more explicitly, syphilis and liver damage killed him). Andre stayed in that location until he finally prostrated himself and begged for God's mercy and forgiveness.

### Memoirs of a Suicide

In another book, *Memoirs of a Suicide*, by the Spirit Camilo Candido Botelho, published in 1955, psychographed by Yvonne A. Pereira, Camilo, who was a famous Portuguese author, committed suicide in June 1, 1890. He writes of the landscape where he found himself:

> "Within its winding gorges and sinister caves, spirits that used to be men and women on the earth howled like hordes of infuriated demons, demented by the absolutely unconceivable intensity and strangeness of the sufferings that tormented them.
>
> In that awful place that distraught eyes of the condemned were unable to discern even the slightest gentle outline of a tree that might bear witness to their hours of desperation; or any comforting scenery, for that matter, that might distract them from the wearisome contemplation of those gorges, where no other expression of life could enter other than that of supreme horror!
>
> The ground, covered with fetid, dark soot-like matter was filthy, pasty, slippery and repugnant! The heavy air was asphyxiating, icy and darkened by threatening clouds, as if never-ending storms were roaring all around. When they inhaled, the spirits confined there would choke, as if the pulverized matter, more noxious than ash and lime, had invaded their respiratory tract, tormenting them with a torture unimaginable to a human mind used to the glorious light of the sun - that celestial gift that blesses the earth every day - and the life-giving currents of salutary breezes that invigorate the physical bodies of the planet's inhabitants."[140]

The absence of the sun, the presence of pitiful creatures, the filth, all in common with both experiences. Not a good place to be. The spirit world must have desired to create a place that would be worse than whatever drove you to the conclusion that death would be a better alternative.

Why does such pain await for suicides and for people who drink, drug, or smoke themselves to death? Because, when we are reincarnated, we are expected to live through our trials, our lessons. The act of dropping out of those classroom activities is not an option.

We are told that when a person commits suicide, they will usually reside in this terrible place for the number of years that they would have normally lived. This is why, we have an obligation to live to our agreed upon lifespan. Since many of us are participants in mapping out the trials we shall experience while incarnated on earth, we have an obligation to stay true to our word and complete what we signed up for.

We must remember, as said many times in books psychographed by Chico Xavier and in the books by Allan Kardec, we are not given trials that we don't have a way to be triumphant. While the road may seem impossible, there is always a method for a successful exit. And by the way, maintain a good attitude throughout the entire ordeal and you may get bonus points.

# Chapter 27 – Reincarnation – What Have we learned

If there is one theme that is present in this book that stands out, I hope it is the feeling that it is not God, Jesus, or the neighbor down the street that judges us, it is ourselves. We are our own judge and jury; the sentences that we hand down to ourselves are stricter than any impartial magistrate would proclaim.

Spiritism deliberately doesn't use the word sin to describe our actions. Why? Although the word sin is a good description for some actions, such as murder, there are activities that many people label as sins that are not in the Doctrine of Spiritism, such as love between two spirits, no matter what sex they are in their present incarnation. Hence, "wrongs" is a better label. Some wrongs are universal and some are personal, such as how we treated one of our family members, to our great regret.

While your behavior may have been perfectly acceptable according to present society, you think back and know that you could have been more sympathetic and helpful. You should have given more of your time and not ignore the pleas of help. These are the realizations that help propel us to a higher level. Don't feel guilty, feel the need for action, to change your behavior the next time. For that is the overarching topic of the book; Reincarnation – there is always a next time.

The laws that should guide us are the laws of Love, Charity, Fraternity and Justice. All nicely summed up in the golden rule, do unto others as you would have them do unto you. For the opposite of the golden rule often succinctly defines our trials, others will do unto us what we did to them.

An example of this is the story of a woman who leaves her husband and children for a lover, then reincarnates and in-turn is left alone, with her children, by her husband. Or the man who steals the inheritance from his brothers and sisters, only to suffer the same fate in the next life, and dies penniless. There is no escape from divine justice, because we are our own jailer, who looks at the situation minute by minute, ensuring we learn through dire calamities, if necessary, and more subtle lessons if appropriate.

Everything is archived in your own conscience, good and bad; your records are always at hand. When you perform a wicked deed, it sits in your conscience like a hot coal and bothers you until the fire is smothered by your future performance. The greatest pain you will suffer in your life is the rebuke of your conscience, which won't recede until you make amends, whether or not the person who was affected forgave you.

Ah, you say, but what about those criminals who don't hesitate to commit horrible crimes, without any perception of guilt, only remorse at being apprehended? Be at ease, these immature spirits, who are not progressive enough to acknowledge the extent of their activities, shall learn their lesson via the trials which await them. Don't be mistaken, all of us, at one time, were mere brutes who took or did what we wanted, because we could. The civilizing lessons of successive reincarnations will eternally succeed. As a mill grinds flour out of coarse wheat, the process of reincarnation turns our malformed and dim spirit into beautiful rays of light, that shine on all of our fellow souls with love.

The population of the world consists of a legion of souls at varied levels of advancement. This is why we still have suffering on this world and will continue in this manner until the earth contains more souls who have realized how to value one another than souls who don't yet possess the sight to understand the effects of their behavior.

Those of us remaining on earth who comprehend the optimal path for improvement are here to lead by example and actively promote respectable conduct. Since we too have lived as reprobates, we have the duty to bootstrap others onto a higher plane.

Keep in mind the end state. There are two major milestones on the horizon. One is personal, the quest for perfection. Each of us must constantly work to expand our spiritual quotient. Doing so in this overwhelming materialistic culture is a major obstacle, therefore each step of progress is a battle well fought. Every time we are able to put our latest acquisition in its rightful order in our priorities, it is one more step toward advancement. Another inch in the climb to the day, when reincarnation is no longer required, only when you are sent on a mission to help others.

The second milestone concerns the future of the planet. Currently the earth is a planet of atonement. Where we are reincarnated to atone for our wrongs and to raise our maturity level so we can be allowed to reside with civilized folks. People, who exist without excessive violence, envy, selfishness and nations seldom engage in warfare to settle differences. A place, that when we are born, we will be able to learn without suffering, for by that time our hard edges would have been filed down. Suffering, the great teacher that concentrates our minds won't be required to alter our preconceptions of right and wrong, for by then we will have honesty and justice ingrained into our beings.

The earth will evolve to a planet of regeneration. Where souls still have something to expiate, may absorb new strength by resting from the fatigue of the struggle. There is still evil, but much reduced, the good outweighs the evil, consequently there is no motive for hatred or discord. The foresight of their future, which is intuitive in the people of these worlds, and the sense of security resulting from a conscience void of remorse, cause them to look forward to death without fear, as being simply a process of transformation, the approach of which they perceive without the slightest uneasiness.

## How do we internalize our new Knowledge?

What does all this mean to us? What are the basic lessons we need to derive from all that has been covered? Much has been exposed to you. If you still have reservations, which is good, please keep reading and searching for your answers. I had many doubts and it took years and numerous dead-ends before I found, what I believe is the truth. Only through your ratiocination processes can you build the foundation of faith. Spiritism, doesn't ask for blind faith, it believes you should think through the alternatives and determine for yourself what are the possibilities and the answers to your questions.

If what you have read strikes a chord with you, then it is so because you already knew the answer, deep down in your sub-conscious, you have lived the process and know it intimately. Now is the moment to bring your new found comprehension to the forefront and make it part of you.

This is the time you can take the knowledge of your trials and use it to move yourself forward. In the book, *Missionaries of the Light*, how we approach our responsibilities is discussed. We are not to think that we must suffer through our educational classes in silence, but think hard how we can use these events to our spiritual advantage:

> "Don't fall into the error assumed by many people. That would imply an obligatory form of spiritual conduct. Of course, individuals are reborn with a relative independence and are sometimes subjected to certain harsher conditions for educational purposes, but such imperative never suppresses the free impulse of the soul in its aim toward advancement, stagnation or fall into lower conditions. There is a plan of spiritually edifying tasks to be fulfilled by spirits who reincarnate, where their guides set the approximate quota of eternal qualities that they are prone to acquire during their transitory existence. The spirit who is returning to the physical realm can either improve this quota and surpass its superior's predictions by means of its own intensive efforts or it can fall short and go further into debt to its neighbor, scorning the holy opportunities that had been granted it."[141]

Hence, our score is up to us, survival shouldn't be enough, only a real triumph should be your goal. And what is the definition of a victory? During each down period, when you are fighting to keep up your physical, mental and spiritual strength, reach down inside and pull out that bit of extra power you have hidden away and determine what could amaze yourself and your friends, incarnate and discarnate, about how well you handled this situation.

Are you able to come out with more wisdom, grace, and calmness? Can you stay happy and upbeat, while conveying the attitude that this is just one more hurdle to surmount in your life? Is it possible to continue to feel for others and take part in their misery while living through your own? Are your thoughts preoccupied with the well-being of your deserving friends instead of focused on your plight?

Oh, how easy it is to write these words and incredibly tough to live them. Who am I, the great whiner through times of trouble, to give advice? Yes, dear reader, take what I say with an air of skepticism. All I can say in my paltry defense is that in my recent past, the overcoming of obstacles has been made so much easier. As if I am gliding over the spikes that lay in front of me. All due to the attitude that I tell myself; OK, I must have planned this and besides pondering, what the heck was I thinking, I try to determine what is the theme of my problems and how can I learn from this?

Secondly, I give thanks for the opportunity to pay my debts, for I probably did some deed to deserve my current situation. Or I must have felt I needed it to accumulate one more valuable lesson in my quest for purity.

For the viewpoint of surveying your life from afar, from the top of the mountain, and visualizing the life you are in, as just one of many is a powerful tool. Whatever mistakes you have made, can be rectified, whatever dreams you have had shattered, can be attained. Whatever bad period you are currently experiencing, is but one small blip. Unimportant and inconsequential for your perpetual climb up the ladder to perfection.

When you sit back and realize the immensity of where you have traveled and look ahead into the vast universe awaiting you, then your earthly troubles recede like the terrain you spot as your aircraft is taking off. What was once large and forbidding is now too small to see in detail, a mountain that has been eroded by time into an anthill.

This is precisely how the impact of reincarnation has upon our lives. We refuse to suffer the little things in life, and after all, against eternity, aren't most items small? We refuse to take part in dishonesty, for to do so would harm others and retard our progress. The momentary monetary gain is nothing compared to the glory which awaits us.

Which is exactly the leverage the spirit world intends for their revelation of the truth of reincarnation to have on us. It pushes us to think large instead of small. To understand the right value to place on material goods and the corresponding weight we should assign to our quest for wealth. For now we should understand, in the depths of our hearts, the relative importance of love, charity, fraternity and justice.

## How do we apply our Knowledge?

Now that you sit upon the mountaintop and see your life; how do you change your behavior to construct a better road to your next destination?

Like any habit you wish to break, it takes time and repetition. Spiritism teaches us that all of our actions begin with our thoughts. Hence, this is where to begin. Start small and determine the easiest counter-productive thoughts to remove from your lexicon.

Pick an object that you wished to have for some time and swirl it around in your mind, what will that object look like in a thousand years. For what purpose did you need it? How will it help you gain wisdom for your climb to perfection? From that angle, ponder for several days or a week and see if the lure of that tie to the material world doesn't loosen. And eventually disappears altogether.

The next exercise is to develop a habit of positive thoughts. For instance, when you are walking down the street and spot a type of person who you have an aversion to. Don't think, there's that person again, how disgusting. Instead, let your thoughts move to the place where you hope that person will find peace in his or her life and is able to finish their trials with success. For you know, like you, they are a student on earth, walking from one class to another, doing their best.

When you see alcoholics and drug addicts, don't curse them as useless under your breath, but think, bless them, for they have made wrong choices and shall return again to fight the battle they must have lost in this round.

Take the opportunity when an accident occurs, where usually you would get mad, calmly think, well that person is learning and I hope they grow from this experience. Help that person understand, to not just feel bad, which is normal, but also the required behavior to deter that event from reoccurring. You will be surprised how your calmness rubs off and affects others around you.

During difficult times with your husband, spouse, or significant other, reflect on why you are with them and how you can assist them in their trials. Don't expect them to mimic your behavior, for that will take time and they must motivate themselves. Therefore, listen to what they have to say and analyze the problem from their viewpoint. Think about your answer from a charitable point of view, what can you do to help, not what can you say to defend yourself. Believe me, this part is extremely difficult, because after all, wouldn't most of us enjoy just a bit of respect? Well, sometimes we just have to forgo it and move on. Besides, it's good practice to increase our humbleness.

Of course your friends may start telling you that you are too passive, too weak, why are you letting others take advantage of you? You may reply that others aren't taking advantage, merely that you have placed problems in their correct order. Worrying about the small things is not on your agenda. If others want their way, so be it, no harm to you. For the important items, such as your honesty and sense of justice, you shall be more firm.

Try peering at life from ten thousand feet up and see how you feel. It is at a very different level from where you have been before. The rocks that are in your way turn to pebbles and the larger obstacles no longer block the road, are actually signposts that a valuable lesson is ahead of you and the choices you make will determine your progression.

Yes, bad events will still affect you deeply, we are human, how could they not? But your recovery time will be shorter and the hours and days lost in self-pity and complaints shall drop considerably. For you have the prescience to pick yourself up, figure out what you just learned and continue on to the next course.

## What should you do next? - Study

The first step is to find out more. Improving your spirituality doesn't just mean feeling more spiritual and less materialistic. It entails the required education to appreciate the workings of the spiritual world and how they interact with us and with each other. When people came to Francisco ("Chico") Xavier to ask after loved ones who passed over, he would also tell them to study Spiritism. For without an understanding of the spiritual realm how can you be sure of what you are working toward and the extent of the rewards which await you?

There are two main places to start; one is *The Spirits Book*, by Allan Kardec. Many people read this book and have their "ah ah" moment, when the spirit world and its processes are exposed, questions that have been in their minds since adolescence are finally answered. Below is a review of Allan Kardec's five books and their content, straight from the Amazon web site introduction for each book;

**The Spirits Book** - Written by Allan Kardec, in 1857, is widely regarded as the most important piece of writing in the Spiritist canon. *The Spirits Book* lays out the doctrine of the belief system. The subjects that Kardec discusses lays down the foundations for the Spiritist philosophy and all of the concepts that would become, and still are, key to the movement's thinking have their genesis in the book. The belief that there is one Supreme Being, God, who created everything in the universe, is postulated. According to the text the Devil does not exist and Jesus is a messenger of God. Although the book does not refer to Jesus as the son of God and no mention is made of the 'immaculate conception' he is considered God's perfect messenger and his teachings are to be adhered to. Reincarnation and the survival of the soul after death are vital beliefs and it is stated that it is through reincarnation that lessons are learnt that can be taken into the next life and that every life moves the soul closer to perfection. According to the book man is made up of three separate elements; the body, the spirit and the spiritual body.[142]

**The Mediums Book** - The Mediums' Book is the second of the five books comprising the Codification of the Spiritist Doctrine. The book presents the teachings of the Spirits on all types of spirit manifestations, the ways of communicating with the invisible world, the different types of mediums, the development of mediumship, and the difficulties and obstacles that may be found in the practice of Spiritism. At the end of the book there is a helpful basic Spiritist glossary. Besides being a source of indispensable reading and research for Spiritists, The Mediums' Book is also an essential source of knowledge for any person interested in the mediumistic phenomenon, which is manifesting increasingly the world over, both inside and outside Spiritist activities per se. Since incarnates are an integral part of the exchange between the two planes of life- the physical and the spiritual- it is advisable that we fully understand the mechanics of such a relationship. The Mediums' Book is the safest guide for all those who have devoted themselves to communicating with the Spirit World.[143]

**The Gospel According to Spiritism** - The Gospel according to Spiritism is the third of the five books that comprise the Spiritist Codification, a compilation of teachings transmitted by high order spirits (the Spirits) and organized and commented on by Allan Kardec. The book contains the essence of the moral teachings of Jesus, thus providing a roof under which followers of all religions- even those who profess no religion at all- can gather, for it offers a sure guide for our inner reform, which, according to Christ, is indispensable for us to find future happiness and inner peace, a state that is possible for the spirit on its evolutionary journey to God only by complying fully with the divine laws.[144]

**Heaven and Hell** – The fourth book of five books, published in 1865. In this book, Allan Kardec approaches divine justice from the point of view of Spiritism. The first part is a comparative analysis of the concepts of different faiths about heaven, purgatory and hell, angels and demons, and future punishment and rewards. The dogma of eternal punishment is especially discussed and refuted by arguments taken from the laws of nature. The second part presents numerous communications with spirits in different situations, and which shed light on the state of the soul after death and its passage from the physical life to the spirit life, which until then had been obscure and feared. It is a sort of travel guide to be used before we enter a new world.[145]

**Genesis** - Genesis is the last of the five basic books of the Spiritist Codification. When studied and understood, it offers a unique opportunity for delving into great themes of universal interest, discussed in a logical, rational and revealing manner. The book is divided into three parts: the first analyzes the origin of planet earth and avoids mysterious or magical interpretations about its creation; the second deals with the question of miracles by explaining the true nature of the fluids and the extraordinary phenomena portrayed in the Gospels; the third part focuses on the predictions in the Gospels, the signs of the times and the new generation, whose advent will be the beginning of a new era for humankind, based on the practice of justice, peace and fraternity. The subjects presented in its eighteen chapters are based on the immutability of the great Divine Laws.[146]

The second book to read, after *The Spirits Book*, is *Nosso Lar*, dictated to Chico Xavier, by the spirit Andre Luiz. The book was psychographed by Chico in the 1940's, during World War II. Psychographed means the process whereby a medium, Chico, writes down what is told to him by a spirit. The name of the spirit, Andre Luiz, is a pseudonym, because he didn't wish for people to start investigating his family. Andre Luiz was a well-off physician who worked in the Rio de Janeiro area. Nosso Lar is his story of dying, waking up in the lower zone and how he came to the celestial city Nosso Lar. He goes into great detail how the heavenly colony works, its rules and the people that reside there.

*Nosso Lar* was also made into a movie; it is in Portuguese, with English subtitles. You can find it for free on YouTube. There are more books by Andre Luiz, in which he reveals further stories about the spirit world and how it watches and guides us every day.

Chico has written more than 400 books, he was attacked by many as being one of a large legion of imposters, whose only aim was to increase his personal wealth. Chico said that he could never fall down, since he never stood up, meaning that he couldn't be charged as a money seeking person because he never took money. All proceeds from his books were donated to charity. As a Spiritist, he knew that selling his services that he received as a gift from God is immoral.

Chico lived in a tiny room with a twin bed. His life style was austere; he spent his whole existence in the service of others. Chico was able to know the future. A person who assisted Chico tells of a time in the mid-1980's when Chico told a group that Brazil would be a major oil exporter and that the oil would be found over five thousands meters under the sea. Everyone silently laughed, they had had plenty of experience of the Brazilian government trying to find oil and nothing ever was successful.[147] Now, of course, Brazil is a major oil producer from fields of oil found out in the deep ocean.

## What should you do next? - Analyze

Now for the fun part; analyze your life, the ups and downs to attempt to discover the overall theme of your current existence on earth. Look back to uncover possible reasons for your trials gives you increased strength to survive future events. For by knowing that you persisted during past hard times, supplies the courage to know that anything ahead of you is also surmountable. Plus, with the certitude that you are responsible for your obstacles, you understand that your trials are there for a reason, that you determined before the physical you was born.

Take, what you believe, to be the major events of your life, list them and then write down what you could have possibly done to deserve this. For example, you had a terrible first marriage. You probably behaved toward your spouse or husband in the same manner as you were treated in your present life. In your next life, your instincts will be fine-tuned to find a sympathetic partner the next time.

In the books by Andre Luiz there are many instances of the consequences of past actions on present lives. That is the problem with a belief in reincarnation, you don't just get the good, an eternity; you also get the work associated with it, learning to be perfect.

# Chapter 28 - Last Words

I would have loved to present more about the destiny of each one of us and the world. There is an abundance of information to discover and explore. The spirit world has sent the human race information via Allan Kardec's five books, Chico Xavier's more than 400 books and other mediums that have psychographed work by various spirits. The last one hundred and fifty years has commenced a quiet revolution, which is only beginning. The full extent has still not been revealed. The material disseminated so far is just the first push, to rebalance the equilibrium between materialism and spiritualism. For English speakers only a small percentage is yet translated. Hence, as each book is translated, new facets of spirit life and methods come to light.

I and others shall be writing more about Spiritism and the possibilities which lie in front of you. Heather Bollech-Fonseca , who currently resides in Florida, has written a brilliant book on how you can live better via Spiritism. You can find it on Amazon; the title is *Changing Lives with Spiritism.*

I intend on revealing more of the plans in the spirit realm for your destiny and the destiny of the world. Not only the strategies laid out by the spirit world, but the process whereby the tasks are accomplished. Understanding the arc of history, the actual causes and effects, the trials and failures of countries and empires is vital for placing ourselves in context of the society in which we have landed.

Whereas, our first priority is our own improvement, our additional duty is to assist our current society and culture to also make progress toward an ideal system based on the Doctrine of Spiritism. Once we view the vast expanse of our past and the trajectories intended for the future, our lives and the associated trials can be seen with greater definition. Above all, we should feel comfortable with the hands that operate the levers that regulate our lives and the future of the planet

I hope as you finish reading what has been presented to you, that it help guides you in your understanding of your greater life. Your life beyond one body, one existence, to use your newfound comprehension to gaze at the long term and find the immaculate goodness and serenity that lies in each one of us. For we all belong to the Supreme Being, the Master Intelligence which sets the laws of nature and enables our journey to perfection.

The aspirations you could never fulfill, the college degree that you had to put off, the trips that you had planned are all still attainable, only postponed for one lifetime. Do not think you are too old to dream of the future; the future is waiting for you. Concentrate on what you want in your next life and the goals to accomplish.

Start considering your new career in the spirit world. What is it that motivates you? What would so fascinate you that you couldn't wait to start and to pursue that avenue for many years? As chronicled in *The Spirits Book*, the possibilities are endless and there are tasks to perform which are beyond imagination.

I will leave you with this message from the spirit Andre Luiz:

> "To receive a body granted by reincarnation is not like being given a boat for a new adventure and being left to chance; instead, it means being given a definite responsibility in the work of learning, elevation or redeeming efforts."[148]

# Your Exploration Continues . . .

Learn more about Spiritism in my blog at:
http://www.nwspiritism.com.

To assist you in understanding more about Spiritism, I have written three other books.

- Explore Your Destiny – Since Your Life's Path is (mostly) Predetermined
- Spiritism 101 – The Third Revelation
- 7 Tenets of Spiritism – How They Impact Your Daily life
- What Really Happens During Near Death Experiences According to Spiritism – 12 NDEs Explained and Explored

In the next sections are the introductions to my books.

Join us on Facebook at: https://www.facebook.com/nwspiritism

Join our discussion group on Spiritism at:
https://www.facebook.com/groups/Spiritist/

Go to the source of Spiritism and read Allan Kardec's books. The two I find most interesting are:

1. The Spirits Book

2. The Gospel According to Spiritism

Follow the life of the spirit Andre Luiz, psychographed by Francisco C. Xavier as he rises to the celestial city of Nosso Lar and he experiences different aspects of how the spirit realm loves and guides us is one of the most satisfying reads in my life. There are thirteen books in the series, only eleven in English at this time, and I urge you to read all of them in order.

1. Nosso Lar

2. The Messengers
3. Missionaries of the Light
4. Workers of the Life Eternal
5. In the Greater World
6. Liberation
7. Between Heaven and Earth
8. In the Domains of Mediumship
9. Action and Reaction
10. Evolution in Two Worlds (not yet in English)
11. Mechanisms of Mediumship (not yet in English)
12. Sex and Destiny
13. And Life Goes On

## Explore Your Destiny – Since Your Life's Path is (mostly) Predetermined

Do you wonder if you have an important call with destiny? That you have been selected for something? A cause of a higher purpose?

Well you have been chosen and the why, when, where and how is the subject of this book.

Your life isn't one of just survival through the daily grind of life. The ups and downs of what you have been through are all for a purpose. Every key experience you have had, every calamity that befell you and each relationship that went south or well are part of your overall story. Each major event in your life has been planned.

Have you felt this could be true? Was there even a hint of recognition that certain events occurred for a purpose? And that you were seemingly on a train headed for some unknown destination and you couldn't get off?

This is because within your deepest thoughts, unconsciously, you recognize that you are part of a greater plan. A plan that has been drawn up with your improvement in mind.

There is an answer to your intuition and questions. The answer is wonderful and your part in the drama you are leading is fascinating. Once you realize the total environment in which you reside in, you will recognize that your life is not dreary, but a heart stopping adventure, a roller coaster ride that drives you forward into an unimaginable future.

*Explore Your Destiny* is divided into four sections. Each section supplies one more piece of the puzzle for you to place, so you can look at your life's arc with new insights.

1. Why – Why are we here and why must we live what we are living through right now? It's the age old expression, that we all say at one time or another, "Why me?" Well there is a reason and it will be explained to you.

2. When – In what period along your souls timeline is all of this happening? Yes, there is a greater context of your soul, which you may not be aware of. Knowing your relative position in the path to perfection will guide you to understanding your current life.

3. How – How does all of this occur? How does the entire process affect your destiny and actions? What are the rules of the game? Knowing the structure and comprehending the basic laws that direct your life provides you with a point of view that will put everything into perspective.

4. Where – Where is this world that plans our destiny? Are there good places to be and are there bad? Where does the earth fit into the logical structure? You will see

> where the regions that you are striving to attain are and where you may be living in your not-to-distant future.

I hope that after reading this book you will have a new view of your life. A view that allows you to look at your circumstances from afar and identify the turning points in your personal destiny. I want you to be in that high level observation tower where you can dispassionately evaluate your life and calmly proceed through the good and bad times. Always keeping your eye on the ball of what your true goal really is – Your triumph in the Spirit and Physical worlds.

My book is available at Amazon; Explore Your Destiny – Since Your Life's Path is (mostly) Predetermined.

**Spiritism 101 –The Third Revelation**

This short book is written as a review of the central concepts of the Doctrine of Spiritism.

**Introduction**

Something wonderful has happened. It occurred in the middle of the 1800's and it caught the attention of the world. It grew quickly in popularity, so fast that many in positions of power went on a crusade to stamp it out.

Why? Because it provided answers to questions that we all have been searching for. Questions that have been posed by philosophers since the beginning of time were asked and the results fully described.

Why such fear by the ruling religious classes? Because it explained the purpose for our life without dogma, without having to ask a priest or reverend for forgiveness. No special clothes to wear, no diet restrictions. No requirement for a specialized building or monthly stipends.

Why was it scorned? Because it didn't use the word "sin". It talked of spirits. It told us we could come back as either sex. And when it was asked about marriage, we were told that marriage is between two spirits, not two sexes.

We were told that a marriage should be the union of two spirits for as long as they work together in harmony. If not, then it wasn't the spirit world that stopped people from parting, it was our erroneous human convictions.

The organized Christian religions reacted strongly. They burned books and harassed those that knew and cherished the fact that the Third Revelation had occurred.

Like other messages of love, charity and fraternity before; this one was met with strong opposition. Ideas are hard to stamp out and this one is growing again. The world is re-awakening to Spiritism.

Learn what Spiritism is and how it can positively shape your life and happiness.

## 7 Tenets of Spiritism – How They Impact Your Daily Life

What are the seven tenets? They are the essential fluid and air in which we swim, walk and run in our daily lives. The seven tenets explain why your life is the way it is and how by realizing the Divine Force that surrounds us is a force for love, you can surmount any obstacle and withstand any ill wind.

Not only survive but prosper. For that is why we are here on earth. To learn, to improve, and to gain experiences. To place in the bottom of your heart that love, understanding, caring and serving are the tools we should use to solve every situation.

Sounds easy but in practice it's difficult. Everyday life swirls constantly around us, as if we live in an eye of a hurricane, and every misstep buffets our emotions. Life is a constant hardship for many. We need to rise above the terrain and visualize the road ahead. From the ground it looks rough and rocky, but from on-high the path appears smooth and the destination closer.

I explore each of the seven tenets and how they have personally affected me and those around me. How they will alter your view of your life and change your outlook and priorities. Giving yourself the seven tenets could be the best present of your life.

The 7 Tenets of Spiritism:

1. We are Immortal Souls
2. God and Jesus Love Us
3. We have Multiple Lives
4. During our Lives We Pay for Past Debts and Accumulate New Experiences
5. We Live and Learn in Close Family Groups
6. Our Destiny is Mostly Predetermined
7. We are Assisted in our Lives by Unseen Spirit Forces

Available at Amazon Kindle in in paperback.

**What Really Happens During Near Death Experiences, According to Spiritism**

12 NDE's Explained and Explored

Why are we interested in Near Death Experiences (NDE)? With the advent of the internet, social media allows masses of people to more efficiently pool together shared experiences than at any other time in history. What was once an isolated phenomenon is now a common occurrence. Whereas, in times past a simple farmer or a rich landowner who would be able to pull back from death, their story, if they chose to tell it, would be a solitary happenstance. Easily explained away or believed. It made no difference, since the significance of the account would be eventually dismissed as an outlying data point.

The recent improvement in the speed and efficiency of human

communication in conjunction with modern medical methods of assisting the human body to recover after trauma has supported the explosion of accounts. And as the interpretations of each individual who returned became widely known and disseminated, others choose to finally reveal their own personal story.

Therefore a small bookshelf of NDEs is now becoming a library. Recollections from every country, culture, language and age group now reside in the great internet cloud. A mountain of data, which can no longer be wished away or ignored. The parallels and common themes from all corners of the world preclude everyone's account to be merely mass hysteria. NDEs aren't in the territory of alien encounters. Doctors, lawyers, professors, engineers, sales and service people are reporting in. Telling us similar refrains, with the added mystery of some NDEs where the person either saw or is told of events that they could not have possibly known in their current state. Taken as a whole, the only conclusion is that something must be happening, beyond our comprehension.

What Really Happens During Near Death Experiences – 12 NDEs Explained and Explored is available at Amazon.

# Author

Stay in touch with the author via:

Spiritist Blog: http://www.nwspiritism.com

Facebook: https://www.facebook.com/nwspiritism

Facebook group to discuss Spiritism: (please request to join)
https://www.facebook.com/groups/Spiritist/

Twitter: https://twitter.com/nwspiritism

If you liked *The Case for Reincarnation – Your Path to Perfection*, please post a review at Amazon.

# Copyright



Version 2016.01.15.01

# Bibliography


Amazon. (2014, May 11). *Genesis*. Retrieved from Amazon Books: http://www.amazon.com/Genesis-Miracles-Predictions-According-Spiritism/dp/8598161780/ref=sr_1_11?s=books&ie=UTF8&qid=1399825900&sr=1-11&keywords=allan+kardec

Amazon. (2014, May 11). *Heaven and Hell*. Retrieved from Amazon Books: http://www.amazon.com/Heaven-Hell-Allan-Kardec/dp/8598161349/ref=sr_1_8?s=books&ie=UTF8&qid=1399825900&sr=1-8&keywords=allan+kardec

Amazon. (2014, May 11). *The Mediums Book*. Retrieved from Amazon Books: http://www.amazon.com/Mediums-Book-Allan-Kardec/dp/8598161829/ref=sr_1_5?s=books&ie=UTF8&qid=1399825900&sr=1-5&keywords=allan+kardec

Amazon. (2014, May 14). *The Spirits Book*. Retrieved from Amazon Books: http://www.amazon.com/Spirits-Book-Spiritualist-Classics/dp/1907355987/ref=sr_1_1?s=books&ie=UTF8&qid=1399825900&sr=1-1&keywords=allan+kardec

Denis, L. (2012). *Life and Destiny*. Forgotten Books.

Dictionary.com. (2014, 03 02). *Dictionary Reference*. Retrieved from Dictionary.com: http://dictionary.reference.com/browse/didactic

Hooper, R. (2007, 2012). *Jesus, Buddha, Krishna & Lao Tzu*. New York: Bristol Park Books.

Kardec, A. (2006). *Heaven and Hell*. Brasilia (DF), Brasil: International Spiritist Council.

Kardec, A. (2008). *The Gospel According to Spiritism*. Brasilia (DF): International Spiritist Council.

Kardec, A. (2009). *Genesis - Miracles and Predictions according to Spiritism.* Brasilia (DF), Brasil: International Spiritist Council.

Kardec, A. (2010). *The Spirits Book.* Guildford, UK: White Crow Books.

Neto, G. L. (2013, June 15). *Remembering Chico Xavier and His Legacy.* Retrieved from YouTube: https://www.youtube.com/watch?v=wY5m3bk0AsY& list=TL01TkXUPh4dbuxLuFJq7Gmn-QZpLdKa5H

Pereira, Y. A. (2012). *Memoirs of a Suicide.* Brasilia (DF), Brasil: International Spiritist Council (EDICEI).

Spiritism. (n.d.). *Wikipedia - Spiritism.* Retrieved September 18, 2014, from Wikipedia: http://en.wikipedia.org/wiki/Spiritism

Swedenborg, E. (1758). *Heaven and Hell.* Europe: A Publice Domain Book.

Swedenborg, E. (2011). *A Swedenborg Sampler.* West Chester, PA: Swedenborg Foundation Press.

Wikipedia. (2014, March 7). *Allan Kardec.* Retrieved from Wikipedia: http://en.wikipedia.org/wiki/Allan_Kardec

Wikipedia. (2014, Dec. 24). *Bezerra de Menezes.* Retrieved from pt.Wikipedia (Portuguese): http://pt.wikipedia.org/wiki/Bezerra_de_Menezes

Wikipedia. (2014, August 21). *Camilo Castelo Branco.* Retrieved from Wikipedia: http://en.wikipedia.org/wiki/Camilo_Castelo_Branco

Wikipedia. (2014, March 7). *Chico Xavier.* Retrieved from Wikipedia: http://en.wikipedia.org/wiki/Chico_Xavier

Wikipedia. (2014, June 26). *Wikipedia - Emanuel Swedenborg.* Retrieved from Wikipedia:

http://en.wikipedia.org/wiki/Emanuel_Swedenborg

Wikipedia. (2014, 11 22). *Wikipedia - Golden Rule*. Retrieved from Wikipedia: http://en.wikipedia.org/wiki/Golden_Rule

Wikipedia. (2015, January 12). *Sleep Paralysis*. Retrieved from Wikipedia: http://en.wikipedia.org/wiki/Sleep_paralysis

Wikipedia. (n.d.). *Wikipedia - Arthur Conan Doyle*. Retrieved September 20, 2014, from Wikipedia: http://en.wikipedia.org/wiki/Arthur_Conan_Doyle

Wikipedia. (n.d.). *Wikipedia - Carl Jung*. Retrieved September 20, 2014, from Wikipedia: http://en.wikipedia.org/wiki/Carl_Jung#Spirituality

Wikipedia. (n.d.). *Wikipedia - Carl Wickland*. Retrieved September 20, 2014, from Wikipedia: http://en.wikipedia.org/wiki/Carl_Wickland

Wikipedia. (n.d.). *Wikipedia - Subtle Body*. Retrieved September 20, 2014, from Wikipedia: http://en.wikipedia.org/wiki/Subtle_body

Wikipedia. (n.d.). *Wikipedia - Synchronicity*. Retrieved September 22, 2014, from Wikipedia: http://en.wikipedia.org/wiki/Synchronicity

Woolworth, T. (2011, February 6). *Thomas Edison's Telephone to the Dead: Myth or Fact?* Retrieved Sept. 20, 2014, from ITC Voices: http://itcvoices.org/thomas-edisons-telephone-to-the-dead-myth-or-fact/

Xavier, F. C. (2004). *In the Domain of Mediumship*. New York: Spiritist Alliance of Books, Inc.

Xavier, F. C. (2008). *The Messengers*. Philadelphia, PA: Allan Kardec Educational Society.

Xavier, F. C. (2008). *Workers of the Life Eternal*. Brasilia (DF) - Brazil: International Spiritist Council.

Xavier, F. C. (2009). *And Life Goes On.* Brasilia (DF), Brasil: International Spiritist Council.

Xavier, F. C. (2009). *In the Greater World.* Brasilia (DF), Brazil: International Spiritist Council.

Xavier, F. C. (2009). *Missionaries of the Light.* Brasilia (DF), Brazil: International Spiritist Council.

Xavier, F. C. (2010). *Action and Reaction.* Brasilia (DF), Brazil: International Spiritist Council.

Xavier, F. C. (2010). *Nosso Lar.* Brasilia - (DF), Brazil: International Spiritist Council.

Xavier, F. C. (2011). *Between Heaven and Earth.* Brasilia (DF), Brazil: International Spiritist Council.

Xavier, F. C. (2011). *In the Realms of Mediumship.* Brasilia (DF), Brazil: EDICEI.

Xavier, F. C. (2011). *On the Way to the Light.* Brasilia (DF), Brazil: International Spiritist Council.

Xavier, F. C. (2013). *Liberation.* Brasilia (DF), Brazil: International Spiritist Council.

Xavier, F. C. (2013). *Sex and Destiny.* Miami, FL: EDICEI of America.

[1] Wikipedia, "Spiritism", n.d., http://en.wikipedia.org/wiki/Spiritism, (accessed September 18, 2014)
[2] ITC voices, "*Thomas Edison's Telephone to the Dead: Myth or Fact?*", n.d., http://itcvoices.org/thomas-edisons-telephone-to-the-dead-myth-or-fact/, (accessed September 20, 2014)
[3] ITC voices, "Thomas Edison's Telephone to the Dead: Myth or Fact?", n.d., http://itcvoices.org/thomas-edisons-telephone-to-the-dead-myth-or-fact/, (accessed September 20, 2014)
[4]Wikipedia, "Arthur Conan Doyle", n.d., http://en.wikipedia.org/wiki/Arthur_Conan_Doyle, (accessed September 20, 2014)
[5] Wikipedia, "Carl Wickland", n.d., http://en.wikipedia.org/wiki/Carl_Wickland, (accessed September 20, 2014)
[6] Wikipedia, "Carl Jung", n.d., http://en.wikipedia.org/wiki/Carl_Jung#Spirituality, (accessed September 20, 2014)
[7] Kardec, A., The Spirits Book, Guildford, UK, White Crow Books, Chap. 4, ques. 166, p. 141
[8] XAVIER, Francisco C. Workers of the Lifer Eternal, Brasilia (DF),EDICEI, p. 365
[9] dictionary.reference.com/browse/didactic
[10] XAVIER, Francisco C. Workers of the Lifer Eternal, Brasilia (DF), EDICEI, p. 365
[11] Kardec, A., The Spirits Book, Guildford, UK, White Crow Books, Chap. 4, ques. 175, p. 144
[12] Kardec, A., The Spirits Book, Guildford, UK, White Crow Books, Chap. 4, ques. 172-173, pp. 143-144
[13] Kardec, A., The Gospel According to Spiritism, Brasilia (DF), EDICEI, Chap. 3, Sect. 17, p. 76
[14] XAVIER, Francisco C. Between Heaven and Earth, EDICEI, pp. 131-132

[15]Wikipedia, "Subtle Body", n.d., http://en.wikipedia.org/wiki/Subtle_body, (accessed September 20, 2014)
[16] XAVIER, Francisco C. Between Heaven and Earth, EDICEI, pp. 132-133
[17] XAVIER, Francisco C. Between Heaven and Earth, EDICEI, p. 136
[18] XAVIER, Francisco C. Between Heaven and Earth, EDICEI, p. 136
[19] XAVIER, Francisco C. Between Heaven and Earth, EDICEI, p. 138
[20] XAVIER, Francisco C. Between Heaven and Earth, EDICEI, p. 139
[21] KARDEC, Allan The Gospel According to Spiritism, EDICEI, Chap. V, Item 11, p. 103
[22] XAVIER, Francisco C. Between Heaven and Earth, EDICEI, p. 180
[23] XAVIER, Francisco C. Between Heaven and Earth, EDICEI, p. 180
[24] XAVIER, Francisco C. Between Heaven and Earth, EDICEI, p. 180
[25] XAVIER, Francisco C. Between Heaven and Earth, EDICEI, p. 181
[26] XAVIER, Francisco C. Between Heaven and Earth, EDICEI, p. 181
[27] XAVIER, Francisco C. The Messengers, Allan Kardec Educational Society, p. 52
[28] XAVIER, Francisco C. The Messengers, Allan Kardec Educational Society, p. 53
[29] KARDEC, Allan The Gospel According to Spiritism, EDICEI, Chap. V, Item 11, p. 103
[30] KARDEC, Allan The Gospel According to Spiritism, EDICEI, Chap. V, Item 11, p. 103
[31] KARDEC, Allan The Spirits Book, White Crow Books, Book 2 , Ques, 383
[32] KARDEC, Allan The Spirits Book, White Crow Books, Book 2 , Ques, 385

[33] KARDEC, Allan The Spirits Book, White Crow Books, Book 3 , Ques, 891
[34] KARDEC, Allan The Spirits Book, White Crow Books, Book 3 , Ques, 385
[35] XAVIER, Francisco C. Between Heaven and Earth, EDICEI, p. 68
[36] Kardec, Allan, The Spiritist Book, White Crow Books, Question 132, p. 121
[37] Pereira, Y. A., Memoirs of a Suicide, EDICEI, p. 289
[38] Pereira, Y. A., Memoirs of a Suicide, EDICEI, pp. 289-290
[39] Xavier, F.C., Missionaries of the Light, EDICEI, pp. 177-178
[40] Xavier, F.C., Missionaries of the Light, EDICEI, p. 164
[41] Xavier, F.C., Missionaries of the Light, EDICEI, p. 179
[42] Pereira, Y. A., Memoirs of a Suicide, EDICEI, p. 424
[43] Pereira, Y. A., Memoirs of a Suicide, EDICEI, p. 424
[44] XAVIER, Francisco C. Missionaries of the Light, EDICEI, p. 171
[45] XAVIER, Francisco C. Missionaries of the Light, EDICEI, p. 179
[46] XAVIER, Francisco C. Missionaries of the Light, EDICEI, p. 173
[47] XAVIER, Francisco C. Missionaries of the Light, EDICEI, p. 173
[48] XAVIER, Francisco C. Workers of the Lifer Eternal, EDICEI, p. 365
[49] dictionary.reference.com/browse/didactic
[50] XAVIER, Francisco C. Workers of the Lifer Eternal, EDICEI, p. 365
[51] XAVIER, Francisco C. Workers of the Lifer Eternal, EDICEI, p. 365
[52] XAVIER, Francisco C. Workers of the Lifer Eternal, EDICEI, p. 365
[53] Pereira, Y. A., Memoirs of a Suicide, EDICEI, p. 9
[54] Wikipedia, "Camilo Castelo Branco", n.d., http://en.wikipedia.org/wiki/Camilo_Castelo_Branco, (accessed August 21, 2014)
[55] Pereira, Y. A., Memoirs of a Suicide, EDICEI, p. 19

[56] Pereira, Y. A., Memoirs of a Suicide, EDICEI, p. 528
[57] Pereira, Y. A., Memoirs of a Suicide, EDICEI, p. 528
[58] Pereira, Y. A., Memoirs of a Suicide, EDICEI, p. 529
[59] Pereira, Y. A., Memoirs of a Suicide, EDICEI, p. 530
[60] Pereira, Y. A., Memoirs of a Suicide, EDICEI, p. 536
[61] Pereira, Y. A., Memoirs of a Suicide, EDICEI, p. 540
[62] Pereira, Y. A., Memoirs of a Suicide, EDICEI, p. 542
[63] Pereira, Y. A., Memoirs of a Suicide, EDICEI, p. 544
[64] Pereira, Y. A., Memoirs of a Suicide, EDICEI, p. 548
[65] Pereira, Y. A., Memoirs of a Suicide, EDICEI, pp. 550-551
[66] Pereira, Y. A., Memoirs of a Suicide, EDICEI, p. 554
[67] Wikipedia, "Leon Denis", n.d., http://en.wikipedia.org/wiki/Leon_Denis (accessed June 6, 2014)
[68] Pereira, Y. A., Memoirs of a Suicide, EDICEI, p. 275
[69] Pereira, Y. A., Memoirs of a Suicide, EDICEI, p. 276
[70] Pereira, Y. A., Memoirs of a Suicide, EDICEI, p. 278
[71] Pereira, Y. A., Memoirs of a Suicide, EDICEI, p. 279
[72] Pereira, Y. A., Memoirs of a Suicide, EDICEI, p. 279
[73] Pereira, Y. A., Memoirs of a Suicide, EDICEI, p. 281
[74] Pereira, Y. A., Memoirs of a Suicide, EDICEI, p. 282
[75] Pereira, Y. A., Memoirs of a Suicide, EDICEI, p. 283
[76] Kardec, Allan, The Spirits Book, White Crow Books, Ques. 999, p. 508
[77] Pereira, Y. A., Memoirs of a Suicide, EDICEI, p. 284
[78] Pereira, Y. A., Memoirs of a Suicide, EDICEI, p. 227 (footnote)
[79] Pereira, Y. A., Memoirs of a Suicide, EDICEI, p. 506
[80] Pereira, Y. A., Memoirs of a Suicide, EDICEI, p. 509
[81] Pereira, Y. A., Memoirs of a Suicide, EDICEI, pp. 512-513
[82] Kardec, A., The Gospel According to Spiritism, EDICEI, p. 86
[83] Kardec, A., The Gospel According to Spiritism, EDICEI, p. 87
[84] Kardec, A., The Gospel According to Spiritism, EDICEI, p. 87
[85] Kardec, A., The Gospel According to Spiritism, EDICEI, pp. 92-92
[86] Kardec, A., The Spirits Book, White Crow Books, Ques. 204, p. 157
[87] Xavier, Francisco C., And Life Goes On, EDICEI, p. 225

[88] Xavier, Francisco C., And Life Goes On, EDICEI, p. 226
[89] Xavier, Francisco C., And Life Goes On, EDICEI, p. 226
[90] Xavier, Francisco C., In the Greater World, EDICEI, p. 178
[91] Xavier, Francisco C., In the Greater World, EDICEI, p. 178
[92] Xavier, Francisco C., In the Greater World, EDICEI, p. 179
[93] Kardec, A., The Spirits Book, White Crow Books, Ques. 488, p. 286
[94] Denis, Leon, Life and Destiny, Forgotten Books, p. 168
[95] Wikipedia, "The Republic (Plato)", n.d., http://en.wikipedia.org/wiki/The_Republic_%28Plato%29 (accessed June 14, 2014)
[96] Wikipedia, "Allan Kardec", n.d., http://en.wikipedia.org/wiki/Allan_Kardec, (accessed May 10, 2014)
[97] Wikipedia, "Allan Kardec", n.d., http://en.wikipedia.org/wiki/Allan_Kardec, (accessed May 10, 2014)
[98] Spirit Writings, "Allan Kardec Biography:, n.d., http://www.spiritwritings.com/kardec.html (accessed May 10, 2014)
[99] KARDEC, Allan. The Gospel According to Spiritism, EDICEI Cap. 5, item 4
[100]XAVIER, Francisco C. Workers of the Life Eternal, EDICEI, pp. 281-282
[101] XAVIER, Francisco C. In the Domain of Mediumship, Spiritist Alliance of Books, p. 34
[102] Global Consciousness Project, "What is the Nature of Global Consciousness", n.d., http://noosphere.princeton.edu/results.html, (accessed May 25, 2014)
[103] Global Consciousness Project, "What is the Nature of Global Consciousness", n.d., http:// http://noosphere.princeton.edu/911formal.html, (accessed May 25, 2014)
[104] XAVIER, Francisco C. In the Domain of Mediumship, Spiritist Alliance of Books, p. 35
[105] XAVIER, Francisco C. In the Domain of Mediumship, Spiritist Alliance of Books, p. 35

[106] XAVIER, Francisco C. In the Domain of Mediumship, Spiritist Alliance of Books, p. 35
[107] XAVIER, Francisco C. Between Heaven and Earth, EDICEI, p. 143
[108] XAVIER, Francisco C. Between Heaven and Earth, EDICEI, p. 143
[109] XAVIER, Francisco C. Between Heaven and Earth, EDICEI, p. 143
[110] XAVIER, Francisco C. Between Heaven and Earth, EDICEI, p. 143
[111] XAVIER, Francisco C. Between Heaven and Earth, EDICEI, p. 144
[112] XAVIER, Francisco C. Between Heaven and Earth, EDICEI, p. 144
[113] XAVIER, Francisco C. Between Heaven and Earth, EDICEI, p. 145
[114] XAVIER, Francisco C. The Messengers, Allan Kardec Educational Society, p. 80
[115] XAVIER, Francisco C. The Messengers, Allan Kardec Educational Society, pp. 80-81
[116] XAVIER, Francisco C. In the Domains of Mediumship, Spiritist Alliance of Books, Inc., p. 128
[117] XAVIER, Francisco C. The Messengers, Allan Kardec Educational Society, p. 81
[118] XAVIER, Francisco C. The Messengers, Allan Kardec Educational Society, pp. 81-82
[119] XAVIER, Francisco C. The Messengers, Allan Kardec Educational Society, p. 82
[120] Swedenborg, Emanuel, Heaven and Hell, Public Domain, section 556
[121] Wikipedia, "Synchronicity", n.d., http://en.wikipedia.org/wiki/Synchronicity, (accessed September 22, 2014)
[122] Wikipedia, "Synchronicity", n.d., http://en.wikipedia.org/wiki/Synchronicity, (accessed September 22, 2014)
[123] Wikipedia, "Synchronicity", n.d.,

http://en.wikipedia.org/wiki/Synchronicity, (accessed September 22, 2014)
[124] KARDEC, Allan The Spirits Book, White Crow Books, Ques, 209
[125] KARDEC, Allan The Spirits Book, White Crow Books, Ques, 573
[126] KARDEC, Allan The Spirits Book, White Crow Books, Ques, 578
[127] KARDEC, Allan The Spirits Book, White Crow Books, Ques, 583
[128] Denis, Leon, Life and Destiny, 2012, Forgotten Books, p. 165
[129] Denis, Leon, Life and Destiny, 2012, Forgotten Books, p. 166
[130] Kardec, A., The Spirits Book, Guildford, UK, White Crow Books, Ques. 261
[131] Kardec, A., The Gospel According to Spiritism, Brasilia (DF), EDICEI, Chap. 16, p. 266
[132] Kardec, A., The Gospel According to Spiritism, Brasilia (DF), EDICEI, Chap. 16, pp. 267-268
[133] Kardec, A., The Gospel According to Spiritism, Brasilia (DF), EDICEI, Chap. 16, p. 280
[134] Kardec, A., The Spirits Book, Guildford, UK, White Crow Books, Ques. 259
[135] Kardec, A., The Spirits Book, Guildford, UK, White Crow Books, Ques. 260
[136] Kardec, A., The Gospel According to Spiritism, Brasilia (DF), EDICEI, Chap. 7, p. 142
[137] Pereira, Y. A., Memoirs of a Suicide, EDICEI, p. 454
[138] Pereira, Y. A., Memoirs of a Suicide, EDICEI, p. 453
[139] XAVIER, Francisco C. Nosso Lar, Brasilia (DF), EDICEI, p. 17
[140] Pereira, Y. A., Memoirs of a Suicide, EDICEI, pp. 19-20
[141] XAVIER, Francisco C. Missionaries of the Light, EDICEI p. 226
[142] Amazon, "The Spirits Book", n.d., http://www.amazon.com/Spirits-Book-Spiritualist-Classics/dp/1907355987/ref=sr_1_1?s=books&ie=UTF8&qid=1399825900&sr=1-1&keywords=allan+kardec (accessed May 11,

2014)
[143] Amazon, "The Mediums Book", n.d., http://www.amazon.com/Mediums-Book-Allan-Kardec/dp/8598161829/ref=sr_1_5?s=books&ie=UTF8&qid=1399825900&sr=1-5&keywords=allan+kardec (accessed May 11, 2014)
[144] Amazon, "The Gospel According to Spiritism", n.d., http://www.amazon.com/Gospel-According-Spiritism-Allan-Kardec/dp/8598161705/ref=sr_1_6?s=books&ie=UTF8&qid=1399825900&sr=1-6&keywords=allan+kardec (accessed May 11, 2014)
[145] Amazon, "Heaven and Hell",n.d., http://www.amazon.com/Heaven-Hell-Allan-Kardec/dp/8598161349/ref=sr_1_8?s=books&ie=UTF8&qid=1399825900&sr=1-8&keywords=allan+kardec (accessed May 11, 2014)
[146] Amazon, "Genesis", n.d., http://www.amazon.com/Genesis-Miracles-Predictions-According-Spiritism/dp/8598161780/ref=sr_1_11?s=books&ie=UTF8&qid=1399825900&sr=1-11&keywords=allan+kardec (accessed May 11, 2014)
[147] Neto, G. L. Remembering Chico Xavier and His Legacy, YouTube, (accessed May 3, 2014)
[148] XAVIER, Francisco C. Missionaries of the Light, EDICEI, p. 23

19743100R00106

Printed in Great Britain
by Amazon